FAITH MARIE BACZKO

THE BLUEPRINT

GOD'S TRANSCENDENT PLAN OF REDEMPTION!

THE HEADSTONE SERIES

BOOK III

A SONG OF ASCENTS - OF DAVID

"I rejoiced with those who said to me,

"Let us go to the house of the LORD."

Our feet are standing in your gates, O Jerusalem.

Jerusalem is built like a city that is

closely compacted together [*united in fellowship*].

That is where the tribes go up, the tribes of the LORD,

To praise the name of the LORD

According to the statute given to Israel.

There the thrones for judgment stand,

The thrones of the house of David.

Pray for the peace of Jerusalem:

"May those who love you be secure.

May there be peace within your walls and

security within your citadels."

For the sake of my brothers and friends, I will say,

"Peace be within you."

For the sake of the house of the LORD our God,

I will seek your prosperity."

Psalm 122 NIV

The Yahweh's House Series is dedicated to my precious son

Jesse Jordan Robinson.

Both Jesse and I have paid the tremendous cost of birthing this

Work in the refining fire of God's Love.

Jesse died on September 10th 2006 in a fatal car accident.

He was twenty- four years old.

The fruit of this Ministry is accredited to Jesse as

his inheritance in Christ

THIS SERIES IS A TRIBUTE TO:

My Heavenly Father, the One to whom I have always been able to run, pour out my heart every day, and receive nothing in return but love. I offer this work back to You Father as a sacrifice of love to be used in the fulfilment of Your plans and purposes.

To Jesus my LORD, my King and Lover of my soul—the One who made it all possible by His precious Blood. Your face is the face I long to see. May these works glorify Your great Name and bring You honour wherever they are taught. Blessing, Honour, Glory and Power belong to You alone, forever and ever for You alone are worthy.

To the most precious Holy Spirit I have no adequate words to describe the depth of gratitude in my heart for You. You have been my Teacher and my Friend during the times I felt alone, my Comforter through the painful times; the One who gently and lovingly encouraged me to keep going when I wanted to quit, and who picked me up and carried me when I could not stand. I do not know how to express how much I love You, but I thank You from the very depths of my heart.

ACKNOWLEDGEMENTS

I wish to thank my Pastors Steve and Sandra Long for their encouragement and support, and for being true reflections of God's love. Thank you being a wonderful example of what it means to be Pastors of God's sons and daughters, and the great example you both are to the Body of Christ, of what great leadership looks like.

I would like to thank Juanita Lubin for her friendship, support and her time spent with me to deal with the issues of my heart.

I would also like to thank Ann Reid, Caroline Phillips and Judy Wilson for being good friends when I needed friends, and for persevering in our friendship.

CONTENT

The Blueprint,

Is also dedicated to the Jewish people

In honour of the nation of Israel;

The crucible in which God has chosen to

Fashion a Body,

Conformed to His Son, Jeshua,

The Hope of Israel, the Desire of all Nations,

To Glorify His Great name

In the Heavens and the Earth.

PREFACE

THE HEADSTONE

"He shall bring forth the *headstone* thereof with shoutings, Crying, Grace, grace unto it." Zechariah 4-7 KJV

The Bride of Christ can be likened to a magnificent Diamond cut and shaped by God the Master Craftsman, design to reflect the multifaceted and multidimensional virtues and attributes of Almighty God. She is His precious Stone, purchased at a great cost to Him. Fashioned and formed under great pressure in the fire of His Love, she emerges a most outstanding, prized and unique stone brought forth for His Royal Diadem for such a time!

Set against the backdrop of the darkness of the world, she lights up in a kaleidoscope of wonder and color. As the fiery Light of His Love touches her, her brilliance shoots forth it's dancing rays of His Great Glory, enticing the world to approach and drink of this great marvel... *"That you may drink deeply and be delighted with the abundance of her glory"*(Is. 66:11).

The Headstone of the temple of God is the Bride incompletion. She represents the fullness of the Glory and majesty of Christ—the perfecting of the work of God in His people. The Headstone corresponds to the Holy of Holies—the Sanctuary the Holy Spirit is now preparing for the Lord's return.

Through the Headstone, the great mystery of God's handiwork throughout the ages is unveiled to principalities and powers; it reveals to all, the manifold wisdom of God and the dynamics of a multidimensional God in perfect union with the 'sons of God.'

There are many important features of the early Church that are presently being restored and God is bringing fresh revelation on key doctrines—all working to prepare the Body of Christ for great moves of God on the horizon. Every work that God has birthed in the past or is presently birthing, to enhance the building work of His House are all important to the completion of His House—each contributes its 'part,' *"For we know in part and we prophesy in part" (1Cor. 13:9).*

The measure that the House of God is structured according to the Father's design—whether individually or corporately—*determines the measure of His Glory it will reflect.* God has been at work over time, building His House, precept upon precept, according to the Body's ability to appropriate and process revelation. With the Body's apprehension of revelation and truth, and a grasp of its identity as *one entity* conformed to the very image of Christ, comes the level of Glory it will appropriate—through God's process the Body is continually moving from one level of the Glory of God to another.

"In Him the whole structure is joined (bound, welded together harmoniously, and it continues to rise (grow, increase) into a holy

temple in the Lord [a sanctuary dedicated, consecrated, and sacred to the presence of the Lord]." Ephesians 2:21 AMP

The Headstone is the culmination of four thousand years of God's work (beginning with Abraham) refined and perfected in the last days in a body of servants. The building of the Headstone is established and purposed to come forth in the Power and the might of the Holy Spirit, in the timing of the apostolic age—the final stage of the building of God's Temple.

The Headstone represents a revolutionary apostolic people led by a God ordained apostolic government united with Christ and firmly established by God. These will work with Him to establish His plans and purposes in the nations through all systems of society in the last days. These servants will walk like Christ, doing and saying only what the Father is doing and saying; they will work with God to prepare the Bride for Union with Christ. The coming forth of the Headstone is Heavens release of a prepared apostolic people who are bold enough to believe God, and to rule and reign with Him *now* to establish His purposes for the ages to come!

The intent of this series is to bring revelation and understanding of *Yahweh's design of His House*—the structure *He intended* to house His Presence and carry the fullness of His Glory. Each of the seven books in *The Headstone Series* represents a facet of Yahweh' House important to its completion, such as Holiness, Israel, women, Heaven's warfare and our identity as sons of God.

God began to download the revelation and understanding of the Headstone in 1993 and released me to write the series between 2000-2004; however, it was only recently in 2012 that He allowed me to prepare the books for publication. Three have been published so far, and I await His timing for the release of the other four.

The Blueprint is the facet of The Headstone revealing the structure of Yahweh's House in relation to His Jewish and Gentile children, and the manner in which this structure has progressed throughout the centuries. It is crucial in these last days to look back to where we have come from, where we are in God's timing and His plans for completing and summing up His work in Christ!

Faith Marie Baczko

INTRODUCTION

"Every valley shall be exalted And every mountain and hill brought low; The crooked places shall be made straight And the rough places smooth; the glory of the LORD shall be revealed, and all flesh shall see it together; for the mouth of the LORD has spoken." Isaiah 40:4-5

The Bride prepared for the coming of the Bridegroom is without spot or wrinkle. As the return of the King draws near, God will ensure that His House is established according to His Blueprint, cleansed and set in order to host His Presence. The Lord is a consuming Fire, faith and obedience are therefore the virtues on which the foundation of His sanctuary is constructed, this in order to sustain the weight of His Glory that is coming.

God's Holy Sanctuary, His Throne of justice and His Seat of mercy can be fashioned only by the Lord. However, God chooses to demonstrate His strength and establish His plans through a people of faith conformed to His image. These are His sons and daughters who walk in the attributes of righteousness, justice and mercy, who carry His anointing, His authority and exude His fragrance.

John the Baptist was such a man, prepared by God to, "Prepare the *way of the Lord*" for His first coming. John was a chosen instrument through whom God worked to prepare the heart of Israel and cleanse it through repentance from sin and dead works. As we approach the time of His *second coming*, the preparation remains the same—*repentance of sin and our dead works carried out in the flesh apart from the direction of the Holy Spirit.*

God is calling a forerunner people to work with Him to prepare the way for the re-entrance of the King of Glory unto planet earth. As we repent of our dead works, we will then be able to perceive and understand His plans, and the blueprint of the sanctuary to which He will return.

God's Blueprint is *Jeshua*! All that He is—His mind, His heart, His attributes, His attitude, His ways and *His chosen form* as the Son and the Root of Israel—is the Plumb Line of the House of God! Sadly, many have committed great atrocities all in the name of Jesus, and sadly, both Israel and the world have judged Jesus and Christianity by those who *claim* to follow Him, rather than allowing His Words and His ways to judge those who make these claims to His Holy Name.

> *"...Yes, the time is coming that whoever kills you will think that he offers God service. And these things they will do to you because they have not known the Father nor Me." John 16:3*

The Blueprint portrays God's unfolding plan of the House He has been at work building over the centuries, a House where He will dwell with man in eternity. The building work began in Israel, and as the Gentile nations are grafted in, it is also completed in Israel.

> *"Then the word of the LORD came to me: "The hands of Zerubbabel have laid the foundation of this temple; his hands will also complete it." Zechariah 4:8-9 NIV*

God has promised in His Word that He will make out of two— the Jewish people and Gentile Christians—one New Man, a New Man that is to become the eternal Dwelling place of God. *The Blueprint* reveals the incredible story of God's plan to bring about this seemingly impossible dream. The plan begins with Abraham, and as it unfolds over history, reveals the detailed Blueprint of the awesome edifice that is Yahweh's House, as it rises in the Glory and Majesty of Christ.

Israel is both a natural and spiritual entity, formed and fashioned by God the Father, as a vessel for the coming of His Son to Earth—"...*a body You have prepared for Me... I have come to do Your will O God*" *(Heb. 10:5-7)*. The Body and vessel in which Jesus chose to tabernacle with mankind, fashioned by the Father, over two thousand years for His first coming, is Israel, "...*the Word was made flesh (Jewish flesh)and dwelt (to tabernacle) among us*" (John 1.14).

However, God's work of building His temple has continued over another two thousand years through both Jewish and Gentile people. It will continue to rise in majesty and Glory to meet the King of kings and LORD of lords at His return in Glory.

The Blueprint is a feeble and humble attempt to portray the unsearchable counsels of the Almighty God of Heaven and earth, in His sublime, transcendent, profound and unfathomable work to create and fashion a place of abode for Himself for all eternity.

Most Holy God, Creator of Heaven and Earth,

I come before you in Your great loving kindness and mercy,

To ask that You would graciously open the eyes, the ears and

The understanding of the reader of this work.

Lord, remove any veil that prevents them

From seeing Your glorious and

Transcendent plan of redemption, as

You have unfolded it over the centuries.

Lord, I plead the Blood of Jesus over all who read this work,

And ask that You would break the power of all anti-Semitic

And religious spirits that would

Seek to hinder Your people from seeing the unveiling of

Your Masterpiece—The Messiah

The Root of David.

A New Man

"I will make you a great nation…

And in you all the families of the earth

Shall be blessed."

Genesis 3:1-3

"The LORD had said to Abram, "Leave your country,

Your people and your father's household

And go to the land I will show you.

I will make you into a great nation and I will bless you;

I will make your name great, and you will be a blessing.

I will bless those who bless you,

And whoever curses you I will curse;

And all peoples on earth will be blessed through you…"

Genesis 12:1-3

1

A New Beginning in a New Land

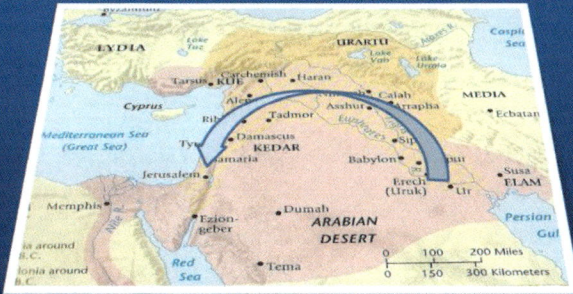

"The LORD had said to Abram, "Leave your country, your people and your father's household and go to the land I will show you. "I will make you into a great nation and I will bless you; I will make your name great, and you will be a blessing. I will bless those who bless you, and whoever curses you I will curse; and all peoples on earth will be blessed through you."
Genesis 12:1-3

The darkest day in the history of humanity, was the day the first created man plunged the world into sin and death. The Earth became corrupted, unclean and defiled in its descent into darkness, giving birth to the spiritual kingdom of Satan. In the Bible this kingdom is referred to as 'Mystery Babylon' rooted in the natural to the dark kingdom of Babylon of that day. Out of this region, from the city of Ur, God called out *another man*. His name was Abraham.

"Get out of your country from your family, and from your father's house, to a land that I will show you." Genesis 12:1

The Father's plan for the redemption of the human race began, when He chose Abraham as the vessel, from whom the prototype of a New Man would be fashioned and formed in the image of His Son. God directed Abraham to leave Ur—symbolic of the kingdom of darkness and the fallen world, and go to a New Land that He would show him. Genesis chapter 12:4 reveals Abraham's heart of obedience and faithfulness, in that he *"...departed as the LORD had spoken to him."* Abraham's heart was being drawn to a City whose Architect and builder was God.

"By faith Abraham, when called to go to a place he would later receive as his inheritance, obeyed and went, even though he did not know where he was going. By faith he made his home in the promised land like a stranger in a foreign country; he lived in tents, as did Isaac and Jacob, who were heirs with him of the same promise. For he was looking forward to the city with foundations, whose architect and builder is God." Hebrews 11:8-10

As Babylon, the land of darkness, bears the image of Satan, the New Land would bear the image of God—Jesus Christ, representative of the Light. Jesus, who is the express image of the Father, is this Land that *"drinks water from heaven"*—the face on the Potter's wheel where the Father's hand would work to shape His New Man and His New Creation called the Heavenly Jerusalem.

In obedience to the LORD, Abraham left the land of darkness in pursuit of God and the land of his destiny. This New Land, chosen by God and separated unto Him for His eternal purposes, therefore became Holy, and is known to this day as the *Holy Land*—the Promised Land of God.

2

A NEW MAN IN THE NEW LAND

Israel My *Son—Prince of God*

"For whom He foreknew, He also predestined to be conformed to the image of His Son, that He might be the firstborn among many brethren."
Romans 8:29

"He said: "Son of man, this is the place of my Throne and the place for the soles of my feet. This is where I will live among the Israelites forever."
Ezekiel 43:7

Martha Charlton

In the New Land, God began His magnificent work of fashioning a New Man and transforming him into a Spiritual being conformed to His image. The Master Potter intentioned that Israel be the clay from which He would mold and form this New Man in His Image—a Man in whom the fullness of God could abide.. Here *within the boundaries of this land* God chose to work to birth a New Creation, *a New Man* and a New Kingdom characterized by the Light of God.

Israel was God's chosen wineskin, prepared as a Body to Host the very Life substance of the Living God, revealed to humanity through

Jesus Christ, *"Therefore, when Christ came into the world, he said: 'Sacrifice and offering you did not desire, but a body you prepared for me...'"* *(Hebrews 10:5).*

Jesus—the Son of God and the Son of Man was sent to the New Land by the Father, to become the prototype for the New Man. Jesus, the Son of God and very God, humbled Himself to be born in this Land as a Man. He became the fulfillment of all the promises of God to humanity.

Jesus became the *Second* Adam and the *First* Fruit of a company as numerous as the stars of heaven—sons and daughters with whom He could commune and have fellowship; a corporate vessel that would one day become united with Him in a holy union of Mind, Heart and Spirit.

"For as in Adam all die, even so in Christ all shall be made alive."
1Corinthians 15:22

"And so it is written, "The first man Adam became a living being." The last Adam became a life-giving spirit. However, the spiritual is not first, but the natural, and afterward the spiritual. The first man was of the earth, made of dust; the second Man is the Lord from heaven." 1 Corinthians 15:45-47

Because of the Lord's sacrifice and through His determination and power, a New Man would emerge from the womb of Israel's travail, conformed to His likeness and fashioned to become the dwelling place and habitation of Almighty God—Yahweh's House.

3

HIS THRONE ESTABLISHED IN THE NEW LAND

"Also your descendants shall be as the dust of the earth; you shall spread abroad to the west and the east, to the north and the south; and in you and in your SEED all the families of the earth shall be blessed." Genesis 28:14

"This is what the Sovereign LORD says:
This is Jerusalem, which I have set in the center of the nations, with countries all around her."
Ezekiel 5:5

God has Purposed that the work to restore humanity to the Father's embrace would be accomplished through the nation of Israel and her Seed—Jesus Christ. His purpose was that through the royal line of the kings of Israel, culminating in Christ, all the families of the earth would be blessed. According to Ezekiel chapter 43:7, God has chosen Jerusalem to be the City of God, the place where His feet would be positioned and His Throne permanently established.

"For the LORD has chosen Jerusalem; He has desired it for His home. 'This is My resting place forever,' He said, 'I will live here, for this is the home I desired. I will bless this city and make it prosperous...'" Psalm 132:13-14 NLT

God's plan of redemption was put in motion, when in the New Land, He set Jerusalem in the midst of nations whose destiny would be determined by their obedience to God, and their relationship to His Land—Israel. Deuteronomy chapter 32:8 states: *"When the Most High divided their inheritance to the nations, when He separated the sons of Adam, He set the boundaries of the peoples according to the number of the children of Israel."*

God decreed Jerusalem to be the Capital of the Promised Land and the centre for all His Kingdom's administrations in the earth—He states in Ezekiel chapter 5:5 *'This is Jerusalem; I have set her in the midst of the nations and the countries all around her."* He declares in Isaiah chapter 2:3, *"The law will go out from Zion, the word of the LORD from Jerusalem."*

Jesus is the King of the Kingdom of God, the seat of whose Throne is Jerusalem. God established Jerusalem and the land of Israel as the central factor, relative to the whole counsel of God, inherent in the plan of God for the redemption of humanity, and the restoration of all things to His original intentions (Acts 3:21).

The Heavenly Jerusalem is the completion of the House begun on the fertile soil of Jacob's life, and whose construction has been taking place over the span of His-story. The Heavenly Jerusalem is the revelation of the Son of God in the fullness of union with mankind. Its gates are constructed in the lives of the twelve tribes of Israel and its walls are built on the foundation of the twelve apostles.

4

THE PLUMB LINE OF THE HOUSE

Faith Marie Baczko

J esus is the Plumb Line the Father has used to test all measures and standards pertaining to His House. *"A plumb-bob or a plummet is a weight, usually with a pointed tip on the bottom, which is suspended from a string and used as a vertical reference line, or plumb-line"* (Wikipedia). The pointed tip of the plumb line is drawn by gravitational force to locate the center of gravity—the law of gravity therefore governs the behavior of the plumb line.

God uses the Plumb Line of Jesus Christ who is the Word of God incarnate, as the foundation and vertical reference of His temple, as it is built upward and rises in Glory to the Throne of God. Jesus' Life is the gravitational pull that forever works to bring all things into alignment to His Standard.

"For God was pleased to have all his fullness dwell in him, and through him to reconcile to himself all things, whether things on earth or things in heaven, by making peace through his blood, shed on the cross." Colossians 1:19-20 NIV

Those who have disregarded the Standard of Jesus' life when attempting to build God's House have produced—similar to the leaning Tower of Pisa, a structure that is off centre or distorted, devoid of the beauty and Majesty of Christ. It is impossible for such a structure to be the eternal habitation of the Everlasting God.

The absolutes of the Word of God must be the Plumb Line of the House that He has designed for Himself, as His place of abode. As the structure goes up God carefully ensures that everything pertaining to His House is true to 'Plumb.' In our quest for God's Glory, the means we use to get to the finish line is as important as the destination.

The absolutes of Christ and God's Word are not intended to limit, but rather to release the freedom found in the resurrection Life of Christ. Our God is a Holy God and He is known in Scripture as the God of patience; throughout history, as man has veered in the wrong direction, away from the Plumb Line, God has continually worked to bring him back to the magnificence of Christ in all His attributes, His features and His DNA.

"Thus He showed me: Behold, the Lord stood on a wall made with a plumb line, with a plumb line in His hand. And the LORD said to me, "Amos, what do you see?" And I said, "A plumb line." Then the Lord said: "Behold, I am setting a plumb line In the midst of My people Israel; I will not pass by them anymore." Amos 7:7

The House that Jesus returns to will be the House that He has designed, built from the Blueprint ordained by the Father and constructed with the substance of Sacrificial Love.

The Foundation Stone

"Thus says the LORD:

'Heaven is My throne, and earth

Is My footstool. Where is the house

That you will build Me?

And where is the place of My rest?'"

Isaiah 66:1

"Behold, I lay in Zion a Stone

For a foundation…"

Isaiah 28:16

5

THE FOUNDATION STONE IS LAID

Yahweh Will Provide The Sacrifice!

"Do not lay a hand on the boy," he said. "Do not do anything to him.
Now I know that you fear God, because you have not withheld from
me your son, your only son." Abraham looked up and there in a
thicket he saw a ram caught by its horns. He went over and took the
ram and sacrificed it as a burnt offering instead of his son. So
Abraham called that place The LORD Will Provide."
Genesis 22:12-14

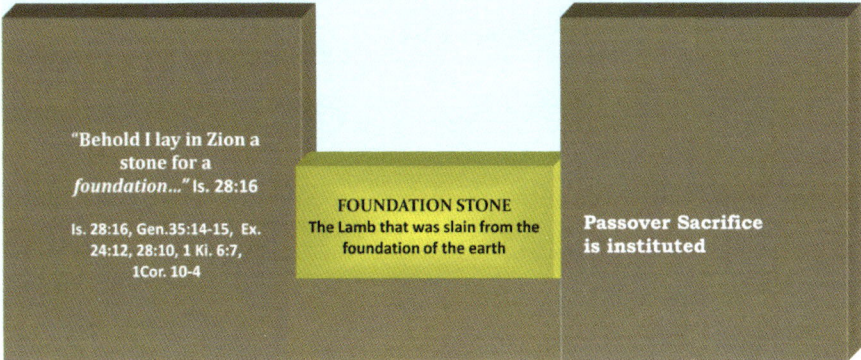

"Behold I lay in Zion a
stone for a
foundation..." Is. 28:16

Is. 28:16, Gen.35:14-15, Ex.
24:12, 28:10, 1 Ki. 6:7,
1Cor. 10-4

FOUNDATION STONE
The Lamb that was slain from the
foundation of the earth

**Passover Sacrifice
is instituted**

I n Abraham, the Father found a man in whom He could proceed
with His awe-inspiring work of fashioning a New Man through
whom He would complete His plans and purposes on earth. God
chose Abraham's seed through Isaac then Jacob, to bring forth the
Man Christ Jesus, through whom all the families of the earth would be
blessed, fulfilling the prophecy that Abraham would become the
father of many nations.

Abraham passed the test when in faith and obedience he was
willing to offer Isaac his only son with Sarah, as a sacrifice unto God.
However, God did not require Abraham's sacrifice—the Father

Himself lays the foundation Stone of His Temple; He had the sacrifice already prepared, a ram representing *His* only Son Jesus, the Lamb slain from the foundation of the earth (Rev. 13:8).

> *"Unless the LORD builds the house, they labor in vain who build it..." Psalm 127:1*

Abraham's obedience released God to lay this stone—the sacrifice of an only son—as the foundation stone of His Temple. The Father laid this stone in the soil of Jerusalem, the place of His heart and the Seat of His Throne. This became the future site of the Sacrifice on the Cross of the Lamb—the Father's only begotten Son, Jesus.

Abraham's act of obedience foreshadowed the Passover Feast, becoming the groundbreaking ceremony and commemoration for the laying of the Foundation Stone of Christ for the Temple of God. This Stone is the Rock of Christ from which Israel drank on their journey in the wilderness, as declared in 1 Corinthians 10:4:

> *"...for they drank of that spiritual Rock that followed them, and that Rock was Christ."*

Jesus was very present with Israel throughout their history. He appears as the angel of the Lord on a journey that would culminate in a collision with his very Presence as the Son of Man and the Son of God (Gen. 22:11, 15).

6

ISRAEL ESTABLISHED IN THE LAND

"You brought a vine out of Egypt; you drove out the nations and planted it. You cleared the ground for it, and it took root and filled the land. The mountains were covered with its shade, the mighty cedars with its branches. It sent out its boughs to the Sea, its shoots as far as the River." Psalm 80:8-11

"When Israel was a child, I loved him, and out of Egypt I called my son." Hosea 11:1

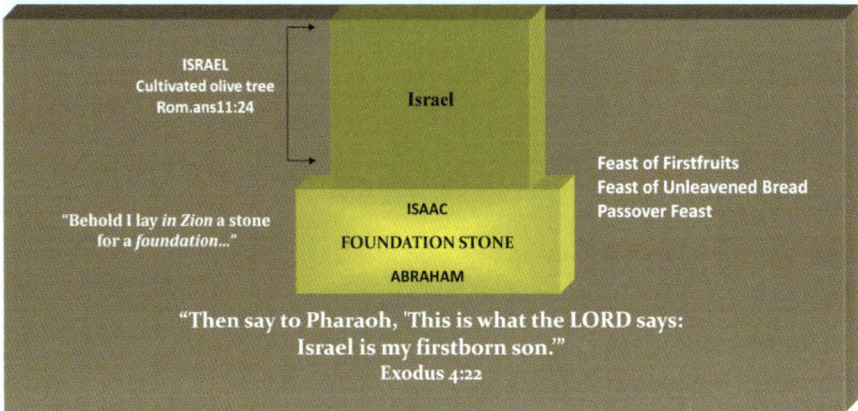

ISRAEL
Cultivated olive tree
Rom.ans11:24

Israel

Feast of Firstfruits
Feast of Unleavened Bread
Passover Feast

"Behold I lay *in Zion* a stone for a *foundation...*"

ISAAC
FOUNDATION STONE
ABRAHAM

"Then say to Pharaoh, 'This is what the LORD says: Israel is my firstborn son.'"
Exodus 4:22

After 400 years of slavery in Egypt, God brought His chosen people out with a mighty hand, and with signs and great wonders, fulfilling the prophecy in Hosea 11:1 that, out of Egypt God called forth *His son Israel.*

God instituted the Passover Feast, founded on the sacrifice of a perfect lamb, when Israel left the land of slavery to life in the Presence of Almighty God. God declares to the world in Deuteronomy chapter 4:34, *"Has any other god dared to take a nation for himself out of another nation by means of trials, miraculous signs, wonders, war, a strong hand, a powerful arm and terrifying acts?" (NIV)*

Through Moses, this terrifying God introduced Himself to a people group for the very first time in history. He claimed them as His own, gave them righteous laws to live by, chose to embrace them in arms of love and taught them the protocol of ministering to, and abiding in the Presence of a Holy and Awesome God.

After forty years in the wilderness learning His ways and being refined in the fire of His Presence, the mighty God of Heaven leads them into the Promised Land of their destiny with signs wonders and great power. God replanted Israel in the Holy Land and established Jerusalem as the place of His Throne, the site where the foundation stone was first laid through Abraham's offering of Isaac.

But you shall seek the place where the LORD your God chooses, out of all your tribes, to put His name for His dwelling place; and there you shall go. There you shall take your burnt offerings, your sacrifices, your tithes, the heave offerings of your hand, your vowed offerings, your freewill offerings, and the firstborn of your herds and flocks. And there you shall eat before the LORD your God, and you shall rejoice in all to which you have put your hand, you and your households, in which the LORD your God has blessed you. Deuteronomy 12:5-7

This site would become the future site where the Temple of God would be established and where Jesus the Lamb of God would be sacrificed. Yahweh's Temple began to rise as He fashions Israel into the vessel through whom He chose to work to bring salvation to the nations of the earth. Jesus declared in John 4:22 that, *"salvation is of the Jews."*

7

THE PASSOVER LAMB IS SACRIFICED

"And so was fulfilled what the Lord had said through the prophet:
"Out of Egypt I called my Son."
Matthew 2:15

"For Christ, our Passover lamb, has been sacrificed."
1 Corinthians 5:7

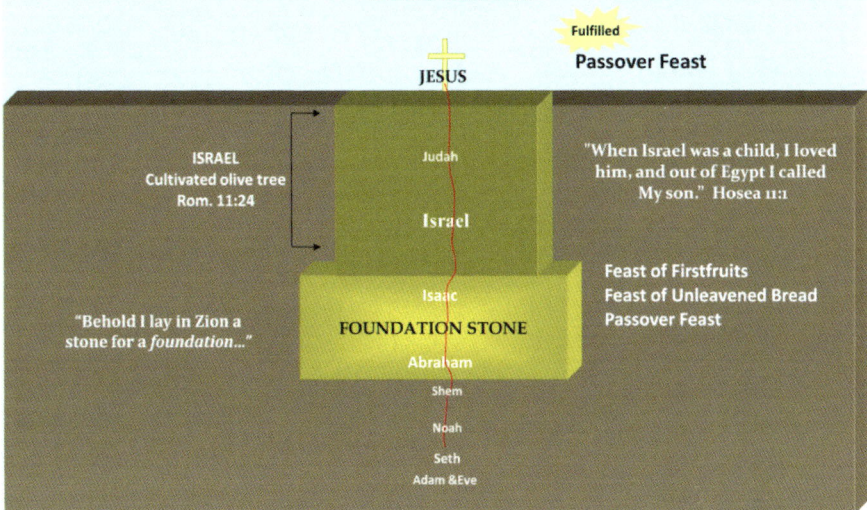

Fulfilled

† JESUS

Passover Feast

ISRAEL
Cultivated olive tree
Rom. 11:24

Judah

"When Israel was a child, I loved
him, and out of Egypt I called
My son." Hosea 11:1

Israel

Isaac

FOUNDATION STONE

Feast of Firstfruits
Feast of Unleavened Bread
Passover Feast

"Behold I lay in Zion a
stone for a *foundation...*"

Abraham

Shem

Noah

Seth
Adam &Eve

Jesus opened the way for Israel and all humanity to be saved
through His obedience to go to the Cross and shed His Blood as
the atonement for our sins.   From the very beginning, and
throughout history God separated a line unto Himself through whom
the Messiah—the Savior of the world, would be born. From Adam's
son Seth to Shem, through Israel to the kings of Judah, God preserved
a bloodline through whom the sacrificial Lamb of God would be born
for the salvation of Israel and the world—the Lion of the tribe *of
Judah.*

"For surely it is not angels he helps, but Abraham's descendants. For this reason he had to be made like them, fully human in every way, in order that he might become a merciful and faithful high priest in service to God, and that he might make atonement for the sins of the people." Hebrews 2:17

Israel was the body fashioned and prepared to birth the King of Kings at His first coming.

"Therefore, when He came into the world, He said: "SACRIFICE AND OFFERING YOU DID NOT DESIRE, BUT A BODY YOU HAVE PREPARED FOR ME... THEN I SAID, 'BEHOLD, I HAVE COME— IN THE VOLUME OF THE BOOK IT IS WRITTEN OF ME— TO DO YOUR WILL, O GOD.'" Hebrew 10:5

The day Jeshua—God's chosen Lamb was sacrificed on the Cross, God's Passover Feast was fulfilled, *"...For indeed Christ, our Passover, was sacrificed for us"* (1 Cor. 5-7).

"...He was led as a lamb to the slaughter, and as a sheep before its shearers is silent, so He opened not His mouth." Isaiah 53:7

The Feasts of the Lord were established by God as *His Feasts.* The celebration of each Feast was His prophetic declaration to Israel and to the world, of key facets of His work to build Himself a House in man individually and corporately.

The multifaceted wisdom of God, the purposes of God, the beginning, the process and the completion of His work, all summed up in Christ, were prophetically declared, and consequently called forth into reality, in the mystery of the ritual and ordinances, practiced year after year, in these seven feasts.

The fulfillment of each Feast marked the completion of a significant phase in the construction of the Temple of God. In Israel's celebration of the Feasts, God, the Alpha and the Omega, was revealing the end from the very beginning. Within these seven feasts, the eternal counsels of God are revealed, and His plan in man and the earth are made complete.

"…and that day about three thousand souls

Were added to them,

And they continued steadfastly in

the apostles doctrine and fellowship,

In breaking of bread and prayers.'

Acts 2:41

THE CORNERSTONE

"The stone which the builders rejected

has become the chief cornerstone."

Psalm. 118:22

"Your dead shall live, together with my dead

Body they shall arise. Awake and sing,

You who dwell in the dust;

For your dew is like the dew of herbs, and

The earth shall cast out the dead."

Isaiah 26:19

8

THE SUPERSTRUCTURE

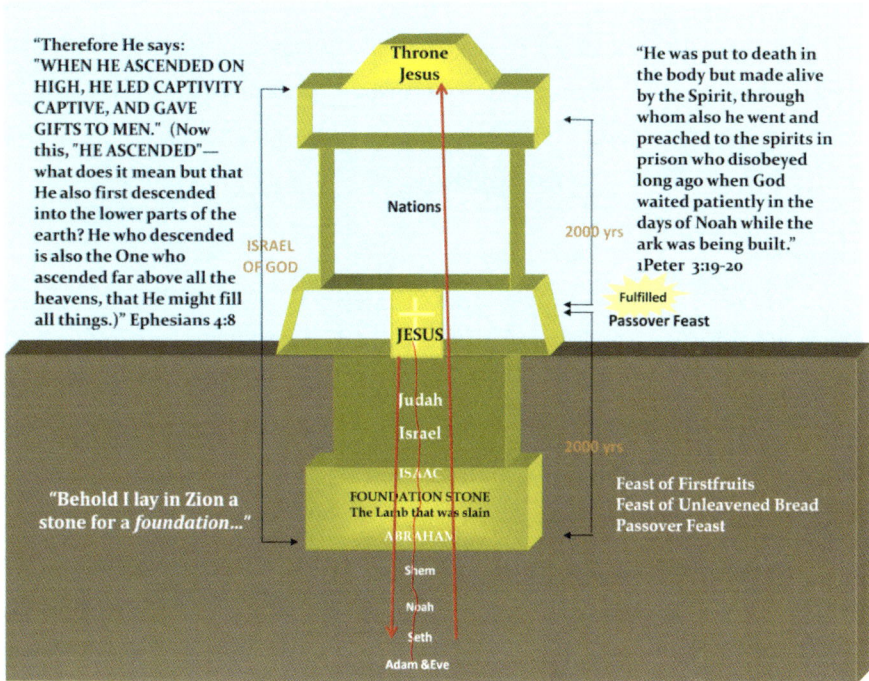

"Therefore He says: "WHEN HE ASCENDED ON HIGH, HE LED CAPTIVITY CAPTIVE, AND GAVE GIFTS TO MEN." (Now this, "HE ASCENDED"— what does it mean but that He also first descended into the lower parts of the earth? He who descended is also the One who ascended far above all the heavens, that He might fill all things.)" Ephesians 4:8

"He was put to death in the body but made alive by the Spirit, through whom also he went and preached to the spirits in prison who disobeyed long ago when God waited patiently in the days of Noah while the ark was being built." 1Peter 3:19-20

Throne Jesus

Nations

ISRAEL OF GOD

2000 yrs

Fulfilled Passover Feast

JESUS

Judah

Israel

ISAAC FOUNDATION STONE The Lamb that was slain

ABRAHAM

Shem

Noah

Seth

Adam &Eve

"Behold I lay in Zion a stone for a *foundation*..."

2000 yrs

Feast of Firstfruits
Feast of Unleavened Bread
Passover Feast

Your dead shall live; together with my dead Body they shall arise. Awake and sing, you who dwell in dust; for your dew is like the dew of herbs, and the earth shall cast out the dead." Isaiah 26:19

After Jesus was crucified, and prior to His resurrection, He descended into the depths where He preached to the spirits in prison and extended salvation to the captives (Ephes. 4:8-10 and 1 Pet. 3: 19-20). In His resurrection these captives were raised with Him, some of whom were seen by many as Matthew 27:52 states:

"...and the graves were opened; and many bodies of the saints who had fallen asleep were raised and coming out of the graves after His resurrection, they went into the holy city and appeared to many."

Ephesians 4: 8 teaches that Jesus led these captives in His train as He ascended to the Throne, this Scripture quoted from Psalm 68: 18, goes on to say *'that He might fill all things.'* The Greek word translated as fill, is the word *pleroo,* which means *to complete or to cram full to completion.*

After the crucifixion, Jesus descended to the foundation of His Temple taking hold of Israel past. He then went further pulling in Adam, Eve, Noah, Shem and all the righteous saints—extending the gift of protection to His natural bloodline through the covering of His Blood. He passed through the heavens and ascended to the highest place, the Throne of God, in order for the Holy Spirit to then be poured out on Israel. Through Israel, the gift of the Holy Spirit was then poured out on the nations of the world, to gather all the chosen of God into the Ark that is 'The Christ,' to cram full to completion His Body—*the Israel of God.*

"For I do not desire, brethren, that you should be ignorant of this mystery, lest you should be wise in your own opinion, that blindness in part has happened to Israel until the fullness of the Gentiles has come in." Romans 11:25

The Cross reaches out in every direction, the past—the righteous of the past, who lived before the Cross, the present and the future—those who have accepted the lordship of Jesus Christ in their lives; all united in the Father's Love through the mercy of the Cross of Calvary

"For God so loved the world that he gave his one and only Son, that whoever believes in him shall not perish but have eternal life." John 3:16

Jesus first 'descended,' then 'ascended' to the place of His Throne—from the soles of His feet to His head, He gave form to His spiritual Body (Ez. 43:7). In His ascension journey to the Throne Jesus' previous cry, "it is finished" became a living reality; His work to complete His Spiritual Body was finished. He filled the whole structure preparing the way for His disciples to make this a reality.

His ascension to the Throne became His final act to bring forth something not previously seen—the Body of Christ—God's Holy Temple.

"For God did not send his Son into the world to condemn the world, but to save the world through him. Whoever believes in him is not condemned, but whoever does not believe stands condemned already because he has not believed in the name of God's one and only Son." John 3:17-18

Jesus fulfilled all the prophecies of the Messiah's first coming; He was born in Bethlehem of a virgin, a son of David, from the tribe of Judah. He was the Lamb of God slain for the salvation of humanity; He was the Son of God and the Son of Man, and would be accepted by the Gentiles (Mic.5:1, Is.7:14, Is.53, Is.11:10, Am. 9:12, Ps.2:7).

"Ya'akov was the father of Yosef, the husband of Miryam, from whom was born Yeshua that was called the Messiah." Mattityahu 1:16 JNT

"For to us a child is born, to us a son is given, and the government will be on his shoulders. And he will be called Wonderful

Counselor, Mighty God, Everlasting Father, Prince of Peace."
Isaiah 9:6

When Jesus returns, all prophecies of the Messiah will be fulfilled and completed in Him. The eyes of Israel will be opened and they will see their Son and their Messiah.

"On that day I will set out to destroy all the nations that attack Jerusalem. And I will pour out on the house of David and the inhabitants of Jerusalem a spirit of grace and supplication. They will look on me, the one they have pierced, and they will mourn for him as one mourns for an only child, and grieve bitterly for him as one grieves for a firstborn son." Zechariah 12:10 NIV

Jesus is returning to the home where He was born, to the land where He once lived and walked with His friends, and His natural family for thirty-three years. Jesus is going home!

"And in that day His feet will stand on the Mount of Olives, which faces Jerusalem on the east. And the Mount of Olives shall be split in two, from east to west, making a very large valley; half of the mountain shall move toward the north and half of it toward the south." Zechariah 14:4

9

THE HOLY SPIRIT BREATHES LIFE

"Suddenly a sound like the blowing of a violent wind came from heaven and filled the whole house where they were sitting. They saw what seemed to be tongues of fire that separated and came to rest on each of them. All of them were filled with the Holy Spirit and began to speak in other tongues as the Spirit enabled them.

...and that day about three thousand souls were added *to them.*"

Acts 2:2-4

"The stone which the builders rejected has become the chief *cornerstone.*"
Psalm. 118:22

APOSTLES

Fulfilled
Feast of Pentecost

ISRAEL
the Cultivated olive tree
Rom. 11:24
JESUS

Passover Feast
Fulfilled

2000 yrs

PROPHETS

Israel

Feast of Firstfruits
Feast of Unleavened Bread
Passover Feast

"Behold I lay in Zion a stone for a *foundation...*"

FOUNDATION STONE

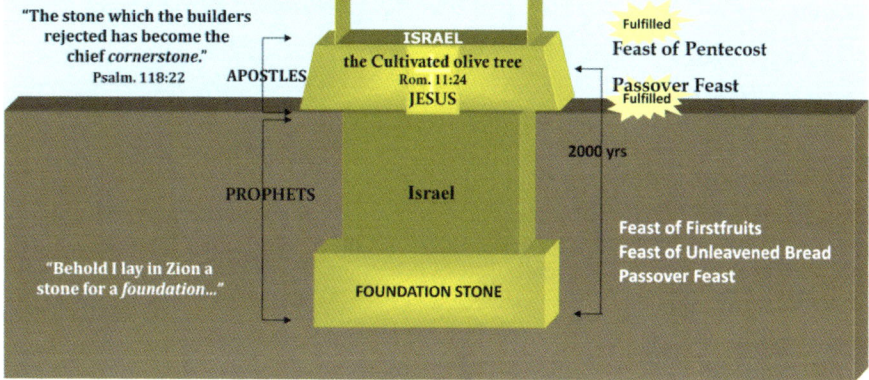

No, this is what was spoken by the prophet Joel: "'In the last days, God says, I will pour out My Spirit on all people. Your sons and daughters will prophesy, your young men will see visions, your old men will dream dreams. Even on my servants, both men and women, I will pour out my Spirit in those days, and they will prophesy."Acts 2:16-18 NIV

After Jesus ascended to the Father, the way was made clear for the Holy Spirit to be released and poured out on humanity. The sacrifice of the spotless Lamb in whom there was no sin, fulfilled the Passover Feast and released the Holy Spirit to breathe the breath of

Life into the Temple, and it became a living breathing entity—a corporate Body indwelt by the Spirit of God.

The Feast of Harvest, also known as Pentecost, was fulfilled with the outpouring of the Holy Spirit, fifty days after the Sacrifice of the Lamb was offered. Through the Father's Gifts to humanity—the sacrifice of His Son Jesus and the giving of the Holy Spirit, He opened a door for a harvest of souls to come into the House of God through the door of Israel.

At Pentecost, the superstructure of the Temple was established in Israel on the foundation of the Jewish apostles and prophets, within the Body of the Jewish King Jesus—*God's* Foundation Stone and now the Chief Cornerstone.

The Olive Tree, that is Christ in Israel, was cultivated by the hands of God from its conception. God began His work with the offering of Isaac by his father, to the Sacrifice of His Son, Jesus, through to the giving of the Holy Spirit, over a period of approximately two thousand years.

The Superstructure that is the Church or *Ekklesia* of God was established in Israel in the City of Jerusalem, by Jewish apostles, with Jewish congregants. The Greek word Ekklesia, simply means the assembly of God; it is the same word used for the congregation of Israel in the Septuagint—the Greek translation of the Old Testament, the apostles and the early church used.

"This is that Moses, which said unto the children of Israel, A prophet shall the Lord your God raise up unto you of your brethren, like unto me; him shall ye hear. This is he, that was in **the church in the wilderness** *with the angel which spake to him*

*in the mount Sina, and with our fathers: who received the lively oracles to give unto us: And behold, the word of the LORD came to him, saying, "This one shall not be your heir, but one who will come from **your own body** shall be your heir." Act 7:37 KJV (emphasis mine)*

God's plan of redemption for Israel still stands and His covenant with them is eternal, as stated repeatedly in His Word:

"And I will establish My covenant between Me and you and your descendants after you in their generations, for an everlasting covenant, to be God to you and your descendants after you." Genesis 17:7

"And so all Israel will be saved, as it is written: "THE DELIVERER WILL COME OUT OF ZION, AND HE WILL TURN AWAY UNGODLINESS FROM JACOB; FOR THIS IS MY COVENANT WITH THEM, WHEN I TAKE AWAY THEIR SINS." Roman 11:26-27

"He remembers His covenant forever, the word which He commanded, for a thousand generations, the covenant which He made with Abraham, and His oath to Isaac, and confirmed it to Jacob for a statute, to Israel as an everlasting covenant." Psalm 105:8-10

On that day I will raise up the tabernacle of David,

Which has fallen down, and repair its damages;

I will raise up its ruins,

And rebuild it as in the days of old;

That they may possess the remnant of Edom,

And all the Gentiles who are called by My name,"

The LORD who does this thing."

Amos 9:11-12

10

THE GENTILES ARE INVITED IN

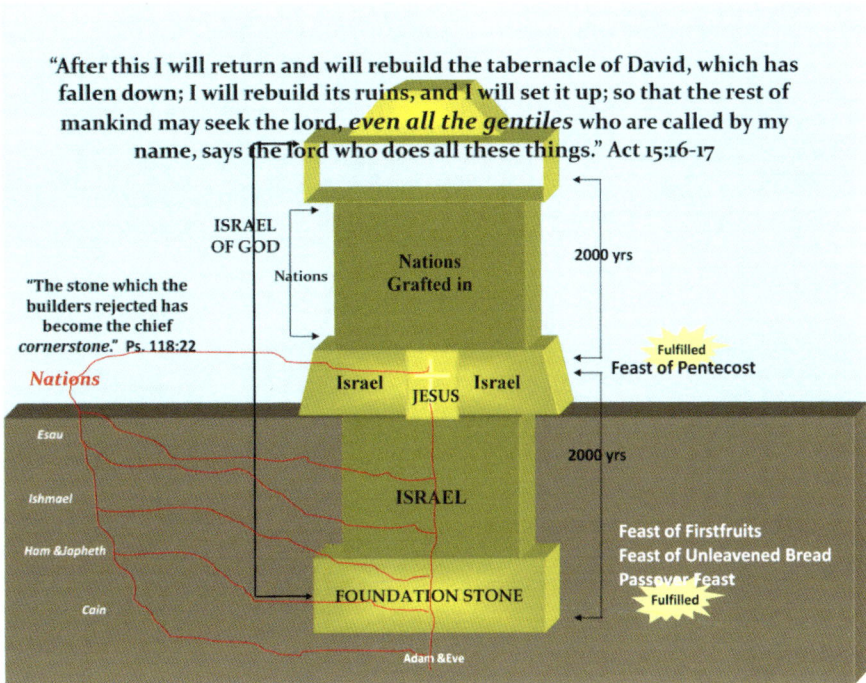

"After this I will return and will rebuild the tabernacle of David, which has fallen down; I will rebuild its ruins, and I will set it up; so that the rest of mankind may seek the lord, *even all the gentiles* who are called by my name, says the lord who does all these things." Act 15:16-17

ISRAEL OF GOD

Nations

Nations Grafted in

2000 yrs

"The stone which the builders rejected has become the chief cornerstone." Ps. 118:22

Nations

Israel   Israel
JESUS

Fulfilled
Feast of Pentecost

Esau

Ishmael

Ham &Japheth

Cain

ISRAEL

FOUNDATION STONE

Adam &Eve

2000 yrs

Feast of Firstfruits
Feast of Unleavened Bread
Passover Feast
Fulfilled

T
hrough the Blood of Jesus, and with the coming of the Holy Spirit, the way was made possible for a harvest of Gentile souls to be grafted into 'the Israel of God' as prophesied by Joel, *"I will pour out My Spirit on all flesh."* The nations were given the opportunity to draw near to God through the covenants and the promises given to Israel and made available through Jesus—the Son of Israel.

At the Jerusalem council that met to discuss the phenomenon of Gentiles receiving salvation in Jesus, James quoted the Word of God spoken through the prophet Amos. Amos prophesied that the

Tabernacle of David would one day be rebuilt, and would become a place where all humanity could seek the Lord. Paul further explains this mystery, hidden even to the prophets in Ephesians 2:11-22.

"Therefore, remember that formerly you who are Gentiles by birth and called uncircumcised....remember that at that time you were separate from Christ, excluded from citizenship in Israel and foreigners to the covenants of the promise, without hope and without God in the world. But now in Christ Jesus you who once were far away have been brought near through the blood of Christ..." (NIV)

Paul further states:

"Consequently, you are no longer foreigners and aliens, but fellow citizens with God's people and members of God's household, built on the foundation of the apostles and prophets, with Christ Jesus himself as the chief cornerstone. In him the whole building is joined together and rises to become a holy temple in the Lord. And in him you too are being built together to become a dwelling in which God lives by his Spirit." NIV

God began His restoration of the Tabernacle of David at the Feast of Harvest (Pentecost), with the outpouring of the Holy Spirit in Jerusalem—the City of David. At this Feast, God began the process of gathering in a harvest of souls, first from Israel and then from the nations. In the mystery of His unfolding will, God established His Church, on the foundation of the apostles and prophets *in Israel,* in Jesus. Salvation is to the Jew first, and the Glory is to the Jew first according to Romans 1:16:

"I am not ashamed of the gospel, because it is the power of God for the salvation of everyone who believes: first for the Jew, then for the

Gentile," and *Romans 2:10: "...but glory, honor and peace for everyone who does good: first for the Jew, then for the Gentile."*

With the outpouring of the Holy Spirit, the nations, drawn by God's love, began to be gathered into the Temple of God through the door of the Cross—a Cross that was driven into the soil of *Jerusalem*— the Holy land, where the Blood of the Son of God was spilled.

In speaking to the nations in Romans chapter 11:17, Paul admonishes the Gentiles not to be arrogant, as we are the wild olive shoot grafted in to Israel—God's cultivated olive tree, cultivated in the soil of His love over a period of two thousand years.

"If some of the branches have been broken off, and you, though a wild olive shoot, have been grafted in among the others and now share in the nourishing sap from the olive root, do not boast over those branches

If you do, consider this: You do not support the root, but the root supports you. You will say then, "Branches were broken off so that I could be grafted in, Granted. But they were broken off because of unbelief, and you stand by faith. Do not be arrogant, but be afraid.

For if God did not spare the natural branches, he will not spare you either. Consider therefore the kindness and sternness of God: sternness to those who fell, but kindness to you, provided that you continue in his kindness. Otherwise, you also will be cut off.

*And if they do not persist in unbelief, they will be grafted in, for God is able to graft them in again. After all, if you were cut out of an olive tree that is wild by nature, and contrary to nature were grafted into a cultivated olive tree, how much more readily will these, the natural branches, be grafted into their **own olive tree**."*

"Now Look at the Jewel I have set before Joshua,

a single Stone with seven facets.

Zechariah 3:9

THE HEADSTONE

"Not by might, nor by power, but by my spirit,

Saith the LORD of hosts.

Who art thou, O great mountain?

Before Zerubbabel

Thou shalt become a plain.

And he shall bring forth the headstone thereof

With shoutings, crying,

Grace, grace unto it."

Zechariah 4:6-7 KJV

"Instead, speaking the truth in love,

We will in all things grow up into Him who is the Head,

That is, Christ.

From Him the whole body,

Joined and held together by every supporting ligament,

Grows and builds itself up in love,

As each part does its work."

Ephesians 4:15-16

11

THE BODY GROWS UP TO THE HEAD

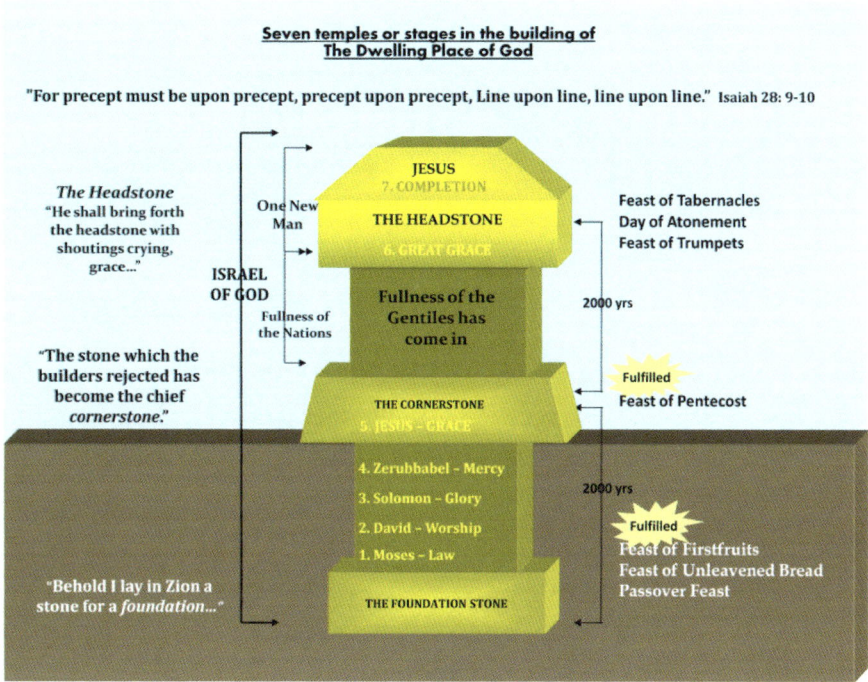

Seven temples or stages in the building of The Dwelling Place of God

"For precept must be upon precept, precept upon precept, Line upon line, line upon line." Isaiah 28: 9-10

The Headstone
"He shall bring forth the headstone with shoutings crying, grace..."

One New Man

ISRAEL OF GOD

Fullness of the Nations

JESUS
7. COMPLETION

THE HEADSTONE

6. GREAT GRACE

Fullness of the Gentiles has come in

Feast of Tabernacles
Day of Atonement
Feast of Trumpets

2000 yrs

"The stone which the builders rejected has become the chief cornerstone."

THE CORNERSTONE

5. JESUS - GRACE

Fulfilled
Feast of Pentecost

4. Zerubbabel - Mercy
3. Solomon - Glory
2. David - Worship
1. Moses - Law

2000 yrs

Fulfilled
Feast of Firstfruits
Feast of Unleavened Bread
Passover Feast

"Behold I lay in Zion a stone for a *foundation*..."

THE FOUNDATION STONE

Yahweh's House is an ongoing work begun by God the Father four thousand years ago on the soil of the life of Abraham, Isaac and Israel. The foundations were established; the superstructure was brought forth at Pentecost, and the foundation of the final phase—*the Headstone*—is now being laid. *'He shall bring forth the headstone with shouts of grace!'* (Zech. 4:7).

Over the centuries, from the time of Abraham, God worked to build precept on precept, in the measure that His people were able to appropriate these truths and principles. He unveiled revelations of Himself, and established His nature, character, and ways into the structure that was to become His dwelling place. Through each of the first five Houses of worship, God laid foundational truths of Himself and His ways into the structure and DNA of His Temple.

Through Moses' tabernacle, He laid the foundation of Law thereby establishing order within the community of His people; through David's tabernacle, He laid the foundations of worship, praise and honor; Solomon's Temple revealed the awesome magnificence, Glory and goodness of the Sovereign Lord, and Zerubbabel's temple revealed the wonderful mercy and faithfulness of a loving God.

To this present day, God has not allowed the rebuilding of another physical temple, as Jesus, Son of God and very God is the House of God—*the fifth temple representing His Grace.* Jesus came as the fulfillment of the Law and representative of all the fullness of God. The Breath of God entered the temple of stone and it became a living breathing entity that is, 'The Christ,' filled with the very Life of God.

Much of the Blueprint of this Temple—'The Christ,' was lost over time especially through the Dark Ages. Over the last 500 years God has been working to restore all that was lost, as we now move into the time of completion and summing up of everything in Christ. The Saints are now being called to return to build the Headstone. This is the last temple or phase, to complete the awesome edifice that is *'The Christ'—the Head and final Stone in holy union with man.*

These temples have all been stages in the work of God over history to build Himself One Magnificent Temple blueprinted in Christ. The last phase will be one that is pure and Holy unto the Lord, built without the defilement of flesh and the carnality of division and prejudice. It will be a Temple without spot or wrinkle that represent Him fully. This one will be the Bride that receives the King in Glory at His Return.

> *"...till we all come to the unity of the faith and of the knowledge of the Son of God, to a perfect man, to the measure of the stature of the fullness of Christ; that we should no longer be children, tossed to and fro and carried about with every wind of doctrine, by the trickery of men, in the cunning craftiness of deceitful plotting, but, speaking the truth in love,* **may grow up in all things into Him who is the head**—*Christ..." Ephesians 4:13-16*

Herod's Temple, restored over forty six years, represented the utter uselessness of flesh, and the futility of man's attempt to build a dwelling for God; this was the temple in question, to which Jesus said, *"destroy this temple and in three days I will rebuild it"* (John 2:19-20). Apart from the wall that still stands today as a reminder of the consequences of abandoning God, this temple was utterly destroyed by the Romans in 70 A.D.

The span of the Temple of God is, the Son of God at the beginning—the foundation and pattern of the Temple; the Son of Man on the Cross at the Crossroads of His-story, drawing into *Agape* love all those who belong to Him by faith, who came before and were to come after; and the Son of God at the end—His Body filled with all the Fullness of the Godhead as He reigns in Glory in union with His Body.

Jesus was at the beginning and He stands victorious in Majesty at the end as *both*, **"the Root *and* the Offspring of David..."** (Rev. 22:16). The Temple of God is Jesus in union with man—Deity in full union with humanity. We are now being called to return and build the Temple as Israel was after seventy years of discipline.

"…till we all come to the unity of the faith and of
the knowledge of the Son of God,
to a perfect man,
to the measure of the stature of
the fullness of Christ…"

Ephesians 4:13

12

COMPLETED IN CHRIST

"Not by might, nor by power, but by my spirit, saith the LORD of hosts.   Who art thou, O great mountain? before Zerubbabel thou shalt become a plain: and he shall bring forth the headstone thereof with shoutings, crying, Grace, grace unto it."
Zechariah 4:6 -7

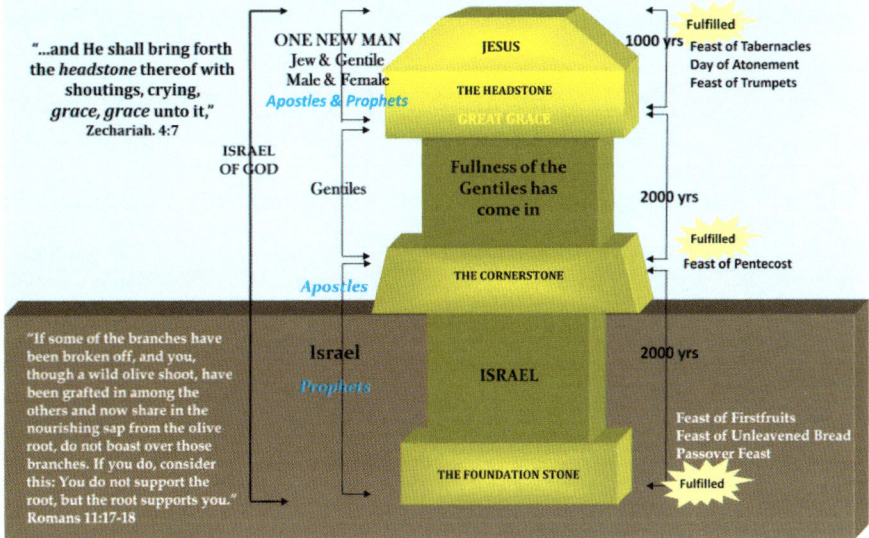

"...and He shall bring forth the *headstone* thereof with shoutings, crying, *grace, grace* unto it,"
Zechariah. 4:7

"If some of the branches have been broken off, and you, though a wild olive shoot, have been grafted in among the others and now share in the nourishing sap from the olive root, do not boast over those branches. If you do, consider this: You do not support the root, but the root supports you."
Romans 11:17-18

ONE NEW MAN
Jew & Gentile
Male & Female
Apostles & Prophets

ISRAEL OF GOD

Gentiles

Apostles

Israel

Prophets

JESUS

THE HEADSTONE

GREAT GRACE

Fullness of the Gentiles has come in

THE CORNERSTONE

ISRAEL

THE FOUNDATION STONE

Fulfilled
1000 yrs Feast of Tabernacles
Day of Atonement
Feast of Trumpets

2000 yrs

Fulfilled
Feast of Pentecost

2000 yrs

Feast of Firstfruits
Feast of Unleavened Bread
Passover Feast
Fulfilled

T he Temple of God built on Hebraic roots is a Man. The Headstone represents a mature Man of the stature of Christ. It is the sons of God built together in union with Christ, *"For in Him we live and move and have our being."*

When the Tabernacle of Moses and the temple of Solomon were completed, both according to God's specifications, the Glory of God descended and filled these temples. When Ezekiel's temple was completed, at the end of nine chapters of specific measurements, God's declaration over it was, *'Yahweh Shamah'—the LORD He is there.*

Jesus Christ is as vast in depth as our forever expanding universe, yet every detail of God's Temple is to be true to Him, nothing is left to chance or to flesh, Romans 11:33 declares, *"O, the depth of the riches both of the wisdom and knowledge of God!"*

Every detail of His first coming—the manner in which He came, the nation and culture He chose to born into—that was the body prepared for Him (Heb. 10:5); the life He lived and walked for thirty three years, the principles that He taught, and His death on the Cross—all are vital parts of the Blueprint of the future habitation of God in corporate Man. If we build *what He built,* He will return to fill it.

No man can build the Temple of God, as its measure is 'The Christ,' and the Holy Spirit alone has the complete Blueprint. Jesus, Son of God and Son of Israel is both the Pattern of the New Man God has been fashioning over the centuries and the Blueprint of the House of God. The measure that the structure we have built, corresponds to the structure He has built, is the measure of the Glory we will appropriate. *God will fill what He builds.*

As we approach the times of the fulfillment of all things, the veil between Heaven and Earth is being progressively removed, as Heaven and an apostolic army of saints unites in the Headstone, under the Headship and government of the King of kings, Jesus Christ.

"And he made known to us the mystery of his will according to his good pleasure, which he purposed in Christ, to be put into effect when the times will have reached their fulfilment—to bring ALL THINGS IN HEAVEN AND ON EARTH TOGETHER under ONE HEAD, even Christ." Ephesians 1:9-10 NIV

We are now living in the times of the restoration of 'all things' as God along with the heavenly hosts work to restore His Temple to the Blueprint of His first intention. The Headstone, that is the last phase of the building work, is God's final work and cover that completes the Temple. The Headstone will come forth in the power of the Holy Spirit, with Great Grace, as God's work in man reaches its fullness through love. The Fullness of Christ in the fullness of times!

"See, the stone I have set in front of Joshua! There are seven eyes on that one stone, and I will engrave an inscription on it,' says the LORD Almighty, 'and I will remove the sin of this land in a single day." Zechariah 3:9

According to Revelation 5:6, these seven eyes represent the seven Spirits of God. The Headstone will characterize the whole counsel of God and will represent the Son of God in fullness as His throne is established in its midst. In these last days, God is working to bring the Body of Christ into a Holy Union with His Mind and His Heart, to be once again caught up in the momentum of His Will.

God is presently releasing His saints from the captivity and the mindset of religious pride and presumption, to build the Headstone according to the blueprint He ordained His Temple two thousand years ago. God's Heart is on His Harvest, He is looking for and expecting a mature leadership to come forth that He might gather in a very great Harvest.

"All by itself the soil produces grain—first the stalk, then the head, then the full kernel in the head." Mark 4:28

ONE NEW MAN

Behold, I will send you Elijah the prophet

Before the coming of the great and

dreadful day of the LORD.

And he will turn the hearts of the fathers to the children,

And the hearts of the children to their fathers,

Lest I come and strike the earth with a curse.

Malachi 4:5-6

"But now in Christ Jesus you who once were far away have
been brought near through the blood of Christ.
For he himself is our peace, who has made the two one and
Has destroyed the barrier, the dividing wall of hostility,
By abolishing in his flesh the law with its commandments
And regulations. His purpose was to create in himself
One new man out of the two, thus making peace,
and in this one body to reconcile both of them to God
through the cross, by which he put to death their hostility.
He came and preached peace to you who were far away
And peace to those who were near.
For through him we both have access
To the Father by one Spirit."

Ephesians 2:13-18

13

ONE NEW MAN COMES FORTH

"And he made known to us the mystery of his will according to his good pleasure, which he purposed in Christ, to be put into effect when the times will have reached their fulfillment—to bring ALL THINGS IN HEAVEN AND ON EARTH TOGETHER under ONE HEAD, even Christ." Ephesians 1:9-10

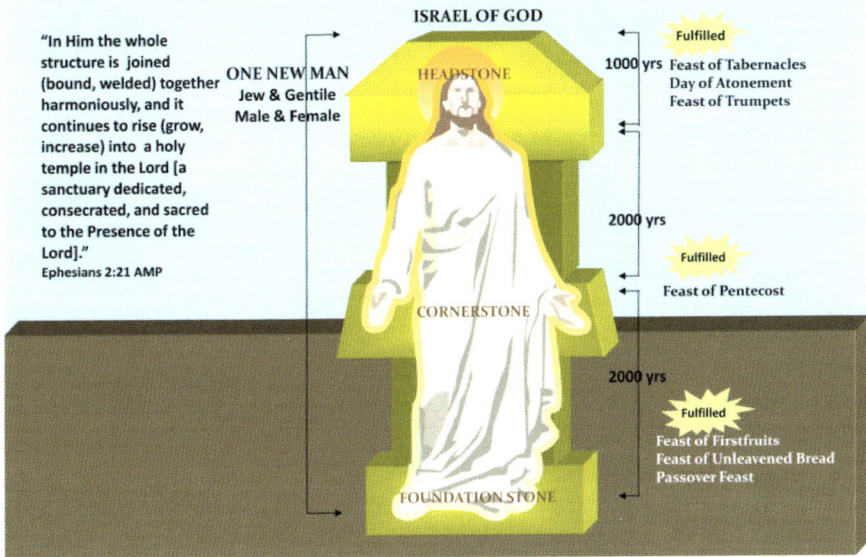

ISRAEL OF GOD

"In Him the whole structure is joined (bound, welded) together harmoniously, and it continues to rise (grow, increase) into a holy temple in the Lord [a sanctuary dedicated, consecrated, and sacred to the Presence of the Lord]."
Ephesians 2:21 AMP

ONE NEW MAN
Jew & Gentile
Male & Female

HEADSTONE

CORNERSTONE

FOUNDATION STONE

Fulfilled
1000 yrs Feast of Tabernacles
Day of Atonement
Feast of Trumpets

2000 yrs

Fulfilled
Feast of Pentecost

2000 yrs

Fulfilled
Feast of Firstfruits
Feast of Unleavened Bread
Passover Feast

God is preparing a chosen Headstone people in these last days to work together with Him to build the Headstone as the cover that will complete His Temple. The whole earth has been awaiting the revelation of these headstone people—'sons of God' who are of the stature of Christ. These sons, comprised of Jew and Gentile, become *one New Man* in union with Christ and the purposes of Christ.

The New Man will give honor to the work God has accomplished in humanity through Israel, as God restores Israel once again as the head and not the tail, and restores Jerusalem as the place of His

Throne and the place of the soles of His feet, where He has chosen to dwell forever (Ez. 43:7).

> *"The hands of Zerubbabel Have laid the foundation of this temple; His hands shall also finish it. Then you will know that the LORD of hosts has sent Me to you. For who has despised the day of small things? For these seven rejoice to see the plumb line in the hand of Zerubbabel. They are the eyes of the LORD, which scan to and fro throughout the whole earth." Zechariah 4:9-10*

The LORD, Yahweh, rejoices when the Plumb Line that is Jesus, the Son of Israel, is in the hands of Israel—the fathers who began the building work on the House of God, the prophets and apostles who have laid all the foundations and principles, and who will work with the Gentile church to complete it. This is God's prophetic word to Israel, a prophecy that He is preparing to fulfill:

> *"Yet now be strong, Zerubbabel,' says the LORD; 'and be strong, Joshua, son of Jehozadak, the high priest; and be strong, all you people of the land,' says the LORD, **'and work; for I am with you,'** says the LORD of hosts. 'According to the word that I covenanted with you when you came out of Egypt, so My Spirit remains among you; do not fear!' "For thus says the LORD of hosts: 'Once more (it is a little while) I will shake heaven and earth, the sea and dry land; and I will shake all nations, and they shall come to the Desire of All Nations, and I will fill this temple with glory,' says the LORD of hosts." Haggai 2:4-7*

God the Father has chosen Israel and the Gentile Christians as vessels through which the Holy anointing oil flows out to touch humanity with His Presence—they are two vessels of oil having one Source, and together they become one in Him.

"What are these two olive trees—at the right of the lampstand and at its left?" And I further answered and said to him, "What are these two olive branches that drip into the receptacles of the two gold pipes from which the golden oil drains?" Then he answered me and said, "Do you not know what these are?" And I said, "No, my lord." So he said, "These are the two anointed ones, who stand beside the Lord of the whole earth." Zechariah 4:14

We have now arrived at the final page of His-story where we must come together in unity to build and prepare the last phase of the Temple—the Most Holy Place—the Headstone of the superstructure. God is now releasing those who will work with Him to complete this last phase of the building work. These are ones with ears to hear; who are willing and obedient; ready to embrace the Cross to follow Him, ready to lay down all of their 'stuff,' ones who are ready to embrace Israel fully. He is now bringing forth His builders—His apostles, prophets, evangelists, teachers and pastors, to work with Him as at the beginning.

The Headstone will be fully represented through the one New Man of both Jew and Gentile, and male and female; it is fashioned in the crucible of Israel, and will be administered through the five-fold ministry of Jesus. The refining and preparation process continues until all have come, *"to the measure of the stature of the fullness of Christ;"* and have grown up *"... in all things into Him who is the head—Christ." (Eph 4:11-16).*

"In Him the whole structure is joined (bound, welded) together harmoniously, and it continues to rise (grow, increase) into a holy temple in the Lord [a sanctuary dedicated, consecrated, and sacred to the presence of the Lord]." Ephesians 2:21 AMP

The Government of God resting on the shoulders of Jesus—the son of Israel and Head of the Body, will be firmly established in the Headstone, in the union of Jew and Gentile in Christ

14

GOD'S GOVERNMENT ESTABLISHED IN ZION

"Many peoples will come and say, "Come, let us go up to the mountain of the LORD, to the house of the God of Jacob. He will teach us his ways, so that we may walk in his paths." The law will go out from Zion, the word of the LORD from Jerusalem." Isaiah 2:3

"Bless God in the congregations,
The Lord, from the fountain of Israel."
Psalm 68:26

The whole issue of Israel and Jerusalem can be reduced to one theme, and that is one of Government. God has chosen Jerusalem as the one location, set in the center of the nations, from where He would establish His Government and administrate His Kingdom. From the very beginning, this has been contested by the kingdom of darkness through the kingdoms of this world. The battle over who will have dominion of the earth, presently raging in the spiritual realm and continually erupting in the natural realm, is centered in Israel.

This is clearly evident in the politics surrounding Israel today—Rome, the Palestinians and the nations under the umbrella of the United Nations, are all vying for power and control over Jerusalem. Israel, the key to the government and rule of the Kingdom of God on earth will remain the center of the battle until the King returns.

> *"Of the increase of his government and peace there will be no end. He will reign on David's throne and over his kingdom, establishing and upholding it with justice and righteousness from that time on and forever. The zeal of the LORD Almighty will accomplish this."* Isaiah 9:7 (NIV)

> *"He will be great and will be called the Son of the Most High. The Lord God will give him the throne of his father David, and he will reign over the house of Jacob forever; his kingdom will never end."* Luke 1:33 (NIV)

> *"At that time Jerusalem shall be called The Throne of the LORD, and all the nations shall be gathered to it, to the name of the LORD, to Jerusalem." Jeremiah 3:17 (NIV)*

> *"For the LORD has chosen Zion; He has desired it for His dwelling place: "This is My resting place forever; Here I will dwell, for I have desired it." Psalm 132:13-14 (NIV)*

Jesus will one day return to planet, earth and many are being called as servants who will work with the Lord to prepare His way. The Government of God, resting on the shoulders of Jesus—the Son of Israel and the Head of the Body, will be firmly established in the Headstone in the union of Jew and Gentile, in Christ.

The Messiah, will return to Jerusalem to fulfill all prophecies and complete God's work. His feet will stand on the Mount of Olives as the Word of God declares (Zech. 14:4), and His Government of the nations will be centered and established in Jerusalem (Is.2:3). Princes will reign with Him in righteousness, and with Him, will rule the nations with a rod of iron (Rev. 2:27, 12:5).

> *"And he who overcomes, and keeps My works until the end, to him I will give power over the nations—'HE SHALL RULE THEM WITH A ROD OF IRON; THEY SHALL BE DASHED TO PIECES LIKE THE POTTER'S VESSELS'— as I also have received from My Father..." Revelation 2:27*

> *"Behold, a king will reign in righteousness, and princes will rule with justice. A man will be as a hiding place from the wind, and a cover from the tempest, as rivers of water in a dry place, as the shadow of a great rock in a weary land." Isaiah 32:1-2*

We do not know the date that He will return, but whatever amount of time that He has given us, it is exactly the amount of time needed to gather in the Harvest, and to make ready the Body of Christ. The final procession of the King into His Sanctuary, as He takes His place on the Throne of God established in Israel, is revealed in Psalm 68:24-35:

> "Your procession has come into view, O God, the procession of my God and King into the sanctuary. In front are the singers, after them the musicians; with them are the maidens playing tambourines. Praise God in the great congregation; praise the LORD in the assembly of Israel. There is the little tribe of Benjamin, leading them, there the great throng of Judah's princes, and there the princes of Zebulun and of Naphtali. Summon your power, O God; show us your strength, O God, as you have done before. Because of your temple at Jerusalem, kings will bring you gifts. Envoys will

come from Egypt; Cush will submit herself to God. Sing to God, O kingdoms of the earth, sing praise to the Lord, Selah to him who rides the ancient skies above, who thunders with mighty voice. Proclaim the power of God, whose majesty is over Israel, whose power is in the skies. You are awesome, O God, in your sanctuary; the God of Israel *gives power and strength to his people. Praise be to God!" (NIV)*

The Hebrew word for assembly in verse 26 is *maqor,* which means, *something dug, a source of water, tears or blood, a fountain.* We are admonished to praise the Lord from the assembly or fountain of Israel, the place from where the Blood of Jesus flowed and the Father's tears were shed for His Son and for humanity. The headwaters of the River of God that began to flow on the Day of Pentecost, is set in Israel. Israel will once again be restored to her place of honor:

> *"Many peoples will come and say, come, let us go up to the mountain of the LORD, to the house of the God of Jacob. He will teach us his ways, so that we may walk in his paths. The law will go out from Zion, the word of the LORD from Jerusalem"* Isaiah 2:3.

When the Government of God is established in Jerusalem through His King Jesus Christ, only then will the nations of the earth have peace! At the return of Jesus to Zion, all the nations of the earth will be required to send a delegation to Jerusalem to worship the King and celebrate the Feast of Tabernacles; if they do not they will experience plagues and will not have rain (Zech. 14:16-19).

As the Return of Jesus draws near this prophecy has begun to be fulfilled in measure, as thousands of saints from the nations of the world go up every year to worship the Lord at this Feast.

The Bride of Christ

"Let us rejoice and be glad and give him glory!

For the wedding of the Lamb has come,

And his bride has made herself ready."

Revelation 19:7 NIV

"…Let the bridegroom go out

from His chamber,

And the bride from her dressing room."

Joel 2:16

15

THE BRIDE IS PRESENTED

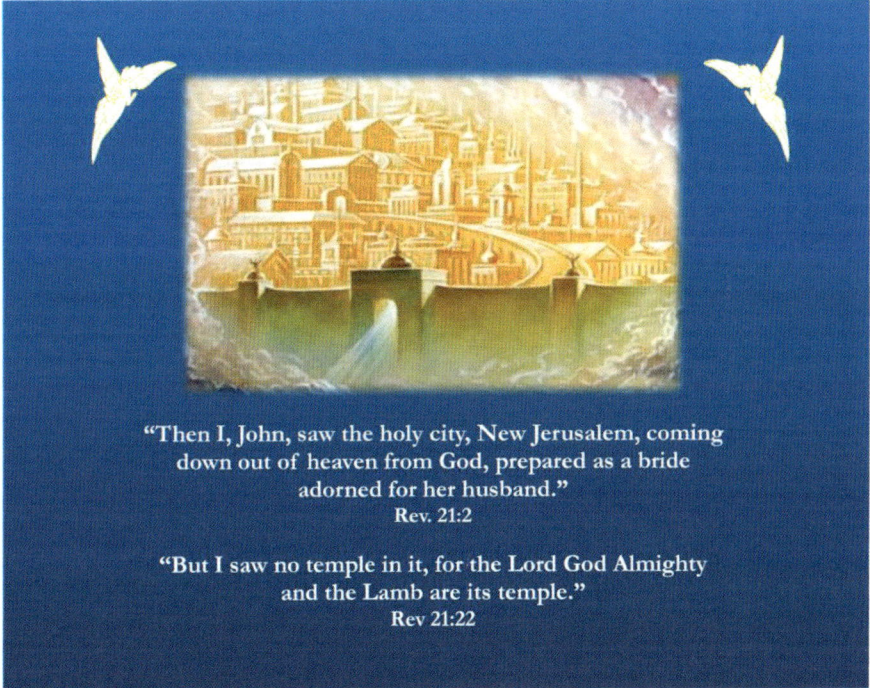

"Then I, John, saw the holy city, New Jerusalem, coming
down out of heaven from God, prepared as a bride
adorned for her husband."
Rev. 21:2

"But I saw no temple in it, for the Lord God Almighty
and the Lamb are its temple."
Rev 21:22

The Majestic unveiling of God's masterpiece, long anticipated before the foundation of the earth is His Bride. A Bride reflected in the sublime mystery of God in union with mankind. She is represented in the Holy City—the New Jerusalem, seen coming down out of Heaven prepared for her Bridegroom.

Jerusalem is representative of God's heart, whenever our hearts are united with God's heart in love, through the Holy Spirit, God's Presence and heart for Jerusalem is manifested. Jerusalem as the

Bride of Christ, is one with the Father and the Holy Spirit. God illustrates His love for Jerusalem in Ezekiel, 16:6-8:

> *"And when I passed by you and saw you struggling in your own blood, I said to you in your blood, 'Live!' Yes, I said to you in your blood, 'Live!' ... I made you thrive like a plant in the field; and you grew, matured, and became very beautiful. Your breasts were formed, your hair grew, but you were naked and bare. "When I passed by you again and looked upon you, indeed your time was the time of love; so I spread My wing over you and covered your nakedness. Yes, I swore an oath to you and entered into a covenant with you, and you became Mine," says the Lord GOD.*

In the Old Testament, Israel and Jerusalem are referred to as God's Bride many times indirectly and seven times directly. In the great body of Church doctrine, laid down in the New Testament Epistles by Paul and the other apostles, the word 'bride' is never mentioned directly, and only once indirectly.

In the Gospels, the word 'bride' is mentioned once in John 3:9 where John refers to Jesus as the Bridegroom and Israel as His Bride; it is mentioned three times in the book of Revelations at the completion of God's work in mankind, summed up in Christ, in the Holy City of Jerusalem.

Every word and detail in the Bible included or excluded is intentional by God, and is with purpose. God's intention for deliberately excluding the word bride from the body of doctrine found in the epistles, may be that Gentiles, who, throughout the history of the Church have been attempting to replace themselves with Israel, might have been given the occasion to do so. The Gentile

Church is the Bride of Christ only as it has been *grafted into* the Bride—the Israel of God. God says of Jerusalem in Isaiah 62:5-7:

> *"As a young man marries a maiden, so will your sons marry you; as a bridegroom rejoices over his bride, so will your God rejoice over you. I have posted watchmen on your walls, O Jerusalem; they will never be silent day or night. You who call on the LORD, give yourselves no rest, and give him no rest till he establishes Jerusalem and makes her the praise of the earth." (NIV)*

The Hebrew word for bride is *kallah,* which means, a *bride – as if perfect,* it is from the root word *kalah* meaning, *to complete and make perfect.* In the times of the summing up of all things in Christ, God will bring Jerusalem, that is the Israel of God—*the one new man of Jew and Gentile*—to completion and perfection, to be unveiled as the most beautiful Bride for His Glory.

> *"The royal daughter is all glorious within the palace; her clothing is woven with gold. She shall be brought to the King in robes of many colors; the virgins, her companions who follow her, shall be brought to You. With gladness and rejoicing they shall be brought; they shall enter the King's palace." Psalm 45:13-15*

Jesus is both the Root and the Offspring of Israel, He is the Alpha and the Omega; He is the beginning and the completion of the Israel of God.

> *"...I am the Root and the Offspring of David, and the bright Morning Star." Revelation 22:16 (NIV)*

In the Glorious City of Jerusalem, the structure that was the Temple of God, so meticulously prepared over four thousand years from the time of Abraham to the return of Christ, is consumed in the

Glory, and has become a Bride. In eternity, the Temple ceases to exist, for the LORD God Almighty and the Lamb are the Temple.

> *"But I saw no temple in it, for the Lord God Almighty and the Lamb are its temple. The city had no need of the sun or of the moon to shine in it, for the glory of God illuminated it. The Lamb is its light."* Revelation 21:22-23

God's intent for both Jews and Gentiles, is contained in His master plan, revealed in Paul's letter to the Romans; chapter 11:29-33 states:

> *"For as you were once disobedient to God, yet have now obtained mercy through their disobedience, even so these also have now been disobedient, that through the mercy shown you they also may obtain mercy. For God has committed them all to disobedience, that He might have mercy on all. Oh the depth of the riches both of the wisdom and knowledge of God! How unsearchable are His judgments and His ways past finding out!"*

After a thousand years of rule on earth, all the carnality and iniquity of the Gentile church and Israel will be consumed in the fire of God's love (1 Cor. 3:15). Everything that could have been shaken, would have been shaken, all that remains of the Edifice of God is the Foundation Stone, the Cornerstone and the Headstone that is 'THE CHRIST!'

The City of God that Abraham longed for is built on the twelve foundations of the apostles who were all Israelites; and the twelve gates leading into the City were honored with the names of the twelve tribes of Israel. God has chosen to give honor to Israel throughout eternity as the little gate through which all who humbled themselves would enter the Holy City.

*"Come, I will show you the bride, the wife of the Lamb."And he carried me away in the Spirit to A mountain great and high, and showed me the Holy City, Jerusalem, coming down out of heaven from God. It shone with the glory of God, and its brilliance was like that of a very precious jewel, like a jasper, clear as crystal. It had a great, high wall with twelve gates, and with twelve angels at the gates. On the gates were written the names of the **twelve tribes of Israel**." Revelation 21:9-12*

"The twelve gates were twelve pearls: each individual gate was of one pearl." Revelation 21:21

He has declared to His people the power of His works,

In giving them the heritage of the nations.

The works of His hands are verity and justice;

All His precepts are sure.

They stand fast forever and ever,

And are done in truth and uprightness.

He has sent redemption to His people;

He has commanded His covenant forever:

Holy and awesome is His name.

Psalm 111:6-9

16

ISRAEL – THE KEY TO THE GLORY

And I will make an
EVERLASTING COVENANT
with them, that I will not turn away
from doing them good;
but I will put my fear in their hearts
so that they will not depart from Me.

Jeremiah 32:40

The Body in which Jesus chose to tabernacle with mankind, fashioned over two thousand years to be His dwelling place, was Israel, *"...the Word was made flesh* (Jewish flesh) *and dwelt among us"* (John 1.14, the Greek word for dwelt means also to tabernacle). The Father had been preparing this Body for Jesus for two thousand years:

Therefore, when He came into the world, He said: "SACRIFICE AND OFFERING YOU DID NOT DESIRE, BUT A BODY YOU HAVE PREPARED FOR ME...THEN I SAID, 'BEHOLD, I HAVE COME— IN THE VOLUME OF THE BOOK IT IS WRITTEN OF ME— TO DO YOUR WILL, O GOD.' "Hebrews 10:5-7

A correct understanding of Israel's significance in the whole counsel of God, summed up in His Son, and the prominence of Israel's place as the key element in the completion of God's purposes on earth, is necessary for our participation in the Father's work of preparing the world for His Son's second coming. God has intricately woven all the events surrounding the return of Jesus to the land of Israel, to His work of the restoration of His chosen people.

Israel suffered judgment and loss because of their unbelief, but God in the mystery of His wisdom saw fit to transform Israel's loss into riches for the world:

> *"But if their transgression means riches for the world, and their loss means riches for the Gentiles, how much greater riches will their fullness bring! ...For if their rejection is reconciliation of the world, what will their acceptance be but life from the dead?"* Romans 11:12 NIV

> *"For, brothers I want you to understand this truth which God formerly concealed but now has revealed, so that you won't imagine that you know more than you do. It is that stoniness, to a degree, has come upon Israel, **until** the Gentile world enters in its fullness; and that it is in this way that all Israel will be saved. As the Tanakh says, "Out of Tzion will come the Redeemer; He will turn away ungodliness from Ya'akov and this will be My covenant with them, ...when I take away their sins."* Romans 11:25 JNT

Do Gentile believers fully comprehend the price Israel has paid, and continues to pay, for giving the world the gift of God's Word and the gift of His Son Jesus? Can anyone fully fathom on this side of eternity the extent of Israel's sacrifice and the riches the world has received because of Israel's loss?

A large percentage of believer's attitudes, ranging from indifference to hatred of the Jewish people, prove otherwise. Nevertheless, God in the mystery of His wisdom transforms the evil the enemy intended into great blessing!

When we pull back the layers of history and look at the mostly hidden story of how God took hold of a small, oppressed people, made them a nation, and deposited His divine principles that have become the bedrock of European and Western Civilization?

"Against all odds, this underdog people have provided the world with its core spiritual and ethical values and a disproportionate amount of modern scientific and social achievements" (Israel Inside).

When Paul states in Romans 11:12, *"How much greater riches will their fullness bring,"* he is referring to the blessing that the world and believers will once again receive, when Israel receives the revelation of Christ and is restored to their Father's embrace. He is referring to the massive explosion of God's goodness and blessing the world and believers will receive when Israel receives the fullness of the Son of God, and He returns to rule and reign over the world.

"For the earth will be filled with the knowledge of the glory of the LORD, as the waters cover the sea." Habakkuk 2:14

The answer to the question of how great will the riches be from Israel's fullness, can be found in the significance of the Greek word *pleroma*, translated also as 'fullness' in verses Romans chapter 11, verses 12 and 25. The word *pleroma* is defined as, *to fill up, what is filled (as a container), and completion.* The name Israel, which means *prince of God*, is the vessel and prepared body of *Jeshua* that believers have been planted into, as stated in verse 17. Gentile believers have been grafted into the Olive tree that is Israel, *with* and *among* the Jewish people, "...*until the fullness of the Gentiles has come in*" verse 25.

Israel is blinded for a season, **until** the entity that is Israel attains fullness and completion, the fullness of believing Gentiles comes in, and Israel and the Gentile church has entered into a true and authentic union. What are the implications of this 'fullness' and completeness for Israel? The *kairos* time, leading up to the Return of Christ—when the fullness of the Gentiles comes in, will be characterized by the ever-increasing Life of Christ, until fullness is attained at His return. Jesus will permeate and fill the whole vessel or Body with the fullness of His Life, His Presence and the full measure of the Holy Spirit.

Jesus' first entrance to earth was to the body of Israel, His second entrance will once again be to the vessel that is Israel:

"On that day his feet will stand on the Mount of Olives, east of Jerusalem, and the Mount of Olives will be split in two from east to west, forming a great valley." Zechariah 14:4

The glorious result of Israel's fullness and completion will be, "The Deliverer will come from Zion and turn away godlessness from Israel"—"And so all Israel will be saved" (Rom. 11:26).

Paul's use of this Old Testament Scripture in reference to the last days reveals that the Deliverer will make His entrance on planet earth through the Beautiful Gate of Israel once again. God is not finished with Israel as some would purport. All movements of God flow from the River of Life, the Headwaters forever established in Jerusalem on the Day of Pentecost. God cannot lie, and His promises to Israel are yes and Amen!

> *"Thus says the LORD, Who gives the sun for a light by day, the ordinances of the moon and the stars for a light by night, who disturbs the sea, and its waves roar (The LORD of hosts is His name):"If those ordinances depart From before Me, says the LORD then the seed of Israel shall also cease from being a nation before Me forever." Jeremiah 31:35 NIV*

Mounting up with the Lord and moving into the realms of His Glory, is the longing of saints who are passionate for their King. God has been revealing many keys to attain to this place of Glory, however, the most significant key the body has been missing, is the great power and authority in the Key of David that opens and no one can shut, spoken of in Isaiah 22:22. This key is a blessing, *forever linked to Israel* through David, who was representative of Jesus, as the Jewish King of Israel.

Those who choose to receive and honor Israel's place as the fathers, are given *this Key* that opens the gates to all the fullness of God's Glory to the Body of Christ—a gate that no man or demon can shut.

The Tabernacle of David holds all the fullness of God and covers all aspects of Christ, as it embodies the King's Sovereign rule over all facets of the kingdom. The throne of Israel is revealed in the Word of God as the Throne of the Kingdom of the Lord over the Israel of God.

> *"And of all my sons (for the LORD has given me many sons) He has chosen my son Solomon to sit on the throne of the kingdom of the LORD over Israel." 1 Chronicles 28:4-5*

He has raised up a horn of salvation for us

in the house of his servant David

(as he said through his holy prophets of long ago),

Salvation from our enemies and from the

hand of all who hate us--

To show mercy to our ancestors and to

Remember his holy covenant,

The oath he swore to our father Abraham:

To rescue us from the hand of our enemies,

And to enable us to serve him without fear

In holiness and righteousness

before him all our days.

Luke 1:69-75

17

HONORING THE FATHERS

They will live in the land I gave to my servant Jacob, the land where your fathers lived. They, their children, and their children's children will live there forever, and David my servant will be their prince forever. I will make a covenant of peace with them; it will be an everlasting covenant. I will establish them and increase their numbers, and I will put my sanctuary among them forever. My dwelling place will be with them; I will be their God, and they will be my people. Then the nations will know that I the LORD make Israel holy, when my sanctuary is among them forever.'" Ezekiel 37:25-28 (NIV)

Hastening the Day of Christ's Return by Honoring the Fathers

"Now if their fall is riches for the world, and their failure riches for the Gentiles, how much more their fullness... For if their being cast away is the reconciling of the world, what will their acceptance be but life from the dead? For if the firstfruit is holy, the lump is also holy; and if the root is holy, so are the branches." Romans 11:13

What will the acceptance of Israel look like and what will their fullness bring to the world? Moreover, to whom is the promise given of *"life from the dead"* in Romans 11:15? By taking the passages in Romans as a whole, I believe the restoration of Israel to their place and purpose in the Father's plan, and their acceptance by Gentile believers, will result in Resurrection life from the dead for the Body of Christ and a massive worldwide awakening!

As a result of the threefold union of Jesus, Israel and Gentile believers, the power of resurrection Life in Christ Jesus, the Head, will be released through His Body. Because of this a New Man will arise in Glory with power to rule and reign over the kingdoms of the earth (Rev. 2:26, Eph. 2:15).

"Life from the dead" is the Body's reception of the fullness of its salvation, as it has grown-up in maturity to union with the Head, and filled with the fullness of resurrection power. This will not occur until the importance of Israel's place in the completion of God's plan is understood, Israel is embraced and honored as the fathers of the Church, and restoration begins.

In recent times there has been much revelation and teaching in the body of Christ concerning honoring the fathers. This movement was initiated by the Holy Spirit, to shepherd all who belong to God, into a union of the Body of Christ, that is holy and pure.

This principle of honoring the fathers is ultimately purposed to find its completion in the restoration of Israel, who are *the fathers* of Christ, and the fathers of the Body of Christ

"Who are the Israelites, to whom pertain the adoption, the glory, the covenants, the giving of the law, the service of God and the promises; of whom are the fathers and from whom, according to the flesh Christ came, who is over all, the eternal blessed God. Amen." Romans 9:4-5

All divisions in the Body of Christ that have taken place through the centuries, beginning with the first in separation from Israel, are now being giving the opportunity for healing and reconciliation that will lead us progressively toward reconciliation with Israel once again.

It is imperative that there be a vital and authentic union between Jew and Gentile—one that produces a New Man, working for the ultimate good and purposes of Christ, to usher in His return to Zion. Through such a union established in honor born of love, the world will then know that the Father sent His Son Jesus into the world for the salvation of mankind (John 17:20).

The union of Israel and the Church is the final breach to be closed for union in the Body of Christ to be complete. God's end-time plans require the closure of this breach, the result of which will be a massive outpouring of His Commanded blessing (Ps. 133). In order to close this breach, we must first look at the root where the breach first occurred and why.

The first division in the church took place when the Roman church took the opportunity to split away from Israel—*the father's of* the Church, in a dispute over the date of the Passover Feast; this decision was made at the Council of Nicea in A.D. 325:

> "From the Letter of the Emperor [Constantine] to all those not present at the council (Eusebius Vita Cons., Lib, III, 18-20):
>
> When the question relative to the sacred festival arose, it was universally thought that it would be convenient that all should keep the feast on one day; for what could be more desirable than to see this festival, through which we receive the hope of immortality, celebrated by all with one accord and in the same manner? It was declared to be particularly unworthy for this, the holiest of festivals, to follow the customs of the Jews, who had soiled their hands with the most fearful of crimes, and whose minds were blinded. In rejecting their customs we may transmit to our descendants the legitimate mode of celebrating Easter; which we have observed from the time of the Savior's passion (according to the day of the week).
>
> We ought not therefore to have anything in common with the Jew, for the Savior has shown us another way; our worship following a more legitimate and more convenient course (the order of the days of the week): And consequently in unanimously adopting this mode, we desire, brethren, to separate ourselves from the detestable company of the Jew.
>
> For it is truly shameful for us to hear them boast that without direction we could not keep the feast. How can they be in the right, they who, after the death of the Savior, have no longer been lead by reason but by wild violence, as their delusion may urge them?...
>
> But even if this were not so, It would still be your duty not to tarnish your soul by communication with such wicked people [the Jews]. You should consider not only that the number of churches

in these provinces make a majority, but also that it is right to demand that our reason approves, and that we should have nothing in common with the Jews, (The Nicean and Post-Nicean Fathers, Vol. XIV, William B. Eerdsman Publishing Company, 1979, pgs. 54-55).

The Roman Catholic Church has since made peace with Israel through the Vatican II conclave concerning replacement theology—the belief that the Church has replaced Israel, and through Pope John Paul II's visit to Israel in March 2000, where he apologized to Israel and prayed at the Wailing Wall. Our intention in quoting this document is by no means meant to bring disrepute on our Roman Catholic brothers and sisters.

However, this document became the initiation of the first division within the Body of Christ—a Body that is holy and precious to the Lord, for whom He gave His very Life. Jesus went to the Cross so that the dividing walls could be removed in His sacrificial love that the two might become One New Man *and* a Holy Bride prepared for His everlasting possession.

The Word of God has shown that Jesus will return in the kairos times of great restoration, ensuring that this breach is repaired, and all things have been reconstituted according to the Blueprint established by God from the foundation of the world.

> *"...and that He may send Jesus Christ, who was preached to you before, whom heaven must receive until **the times of restoration of all things,** which God has spoken by the mouth of all His holy prophets since the world began." Acts 3:20-21*

The Greek Word used in this Scripture as restoration is *apokatastasis,* which means *reconstitution* or *restitution.* The definition of reconstitution is to *reconstruct;* this word also means *to return from a dehydrated state to a liquid stated by adding water.* Restitution is defined as *the restoration of rights, or property previously taken away; restoration to the former or original state or position.* It also means, *recompense, make amends and compensate.*

Before the return of Christ, the Father will see to it that the House of God is reconstructed and restored to His original intention in obedience to the commands given in His Word. With the outpouring of the water of His Word and the outpouring of the Holy Spirit, the dehydrated Body of Christ will be restored to Life.

God commanded that *His Feasts* were to be held on certain dates, as these dates were significantly related to specific purposes and events. *The date of the Passover Feast, and all seven Feasts, were established by God in the Word of God for specific reasons, and are unchangeable.*

> *"Speak to the children of Israel, and say to them: 'The feasts of the LORD, which you shall proclaim to be holy convocations, these are My feasts... 'These are the feasts of the LORD, holy convocations which you shall proclaim at their appointed times. On the fourteenth day of the first month at twilight is the LORD's Passover." Leviticus 23:2-5*

Jesus *"our Passover"* (1Cor.5:7), was crucified on a specific date ordained by God—*during the Passover Feast on the day the lamb was sacrificed.* This signified an end to the dispensation of Law, and our Passover into the dispensation of Grace. The outpouring of the Holy Spirit also fell on a specific date ordained by God—fifty days after Passover, *at the Feast of Pentecost.*

Because God ordained specific dates to hold each of His Feasts, it is only reasonable to expect that the dates for the feasts yet to be fulfilled, are also important and vital in His purposes, as His plans continue to unfold.

The Gentile church chose to change the date of the time that *Jesus the Lamb was slain,* from the time of the *Passover Feast* to a time called Easter—a pagan festival; this has therefore changed the date of Pentecost which was to be held fifty days later. God has been very merciful and gracious, and has even had His purposes in allowing the Gentile church to change the dates of His Feasts, *for a season.*

As '*the fullness of the Gentiles comes in*' to the Israel of God, and as we approach the end of the age—the time of the summing up of all things in Christ, and the restoration of all things—it will become increasingly important for the Body of Christ to return to giving honor to the dates ordained by God the Father.

There are many good reasons for honoring the original dates; first, to honor God's Word and restore things to *His* order; secondly, to honor Israel, to *"turn the hearts of the children to the fathers and the fathers to the children,"* and lastly because these are the dates Jesus will honor when He returns. The Passover and the Feast of Tabernacles are two feast that will be celebrated during Jesus' reign on earth (Ez. 45:21, Zech, 12.14:16).

Honoring the original dates set by God will be an important act in the healing and closing of the breach between Israel and the Gentile Church, as this is the root where the division first came in. Closure of this breach will facilitate the union of both in Christ—*our Passover.*

God will send His servants in the spirit of Elijah to prepare the way of the Lord, and turn the heart of the fathers to the children and the children to the fathers. The consequences of disobedience to God's will is dire for us and for the world.

"Behold, I will send you Elijah the prophet before the coming of the great and dreadful day of the LORD. and he will turn the hearts of the fathers to the children, and the hearts of the children to their fathers, lest I come and strike the earth with a curse."Malachi 4:6

We can hasten the day of the Lord's return by seeking to be connected to Israel in an authentic way—by honoring and loving the Jewish people for the price they have paid. It is time now to work with the Lord to see Israel restored and established in the fullness of their calling, pray and intercede for them, and support them as we are admonished to:

"For if the Gentiles have shared in the Jews' spiritual blessings, they owe it to the Jews to share with them their material blessings" Romans 15:26-27

If we truly love the Lord and seek His will above ours we will seek to be a blessing to the chosen people of Israel.

"Pray for the peace of Jerusalem. For the sake of my brethren and companions, I will now say, "Peace be within you."

Because of the House of the Lord our God, I will seek your good."

Psalm 122:6-9

18

ONE UNITED MAN

Christine Peterkin

Since establishing His Church in Christ on the foundation of Israel, God has been at work in the Gentile nations, for two thousand years. This may seem like a very long time, and may have given the impression that God is finished with Israel, but a thousand years is a day to the Lord (2Pet. 3:8). God spent close to two thousand years, from the time of Abraham, cultivating the Olive Tree that is Israel, to prepare it to receive the grafting in of Gentiles(Rom. 11)—in God's use of numbers four is the number of the New Creation.

God is now making the necessary preparations to move into the final phase of His work, where His eyes are centered once again on Israel, as Israel awakens once again to their God.

> *"By Abolishing in His [own crucified] flesh the enmity [caused by] the Law with its decrees and ordinances [which He annulled]; that He from the two might create in Himself one new man [One new quality of humanity out of the two], so masking peace. And [He designed] to reconcile to God both [Jew and Gentile, united] in a single body by means of His cross, thereby killing the mutual enmity and bringing the feud to an end." Ephesians 2:15-16 AMP*

Jesus became a stumbling block to Israel, but Israel has also become a stumbling block to the Church. In this last phase of His work, He will remove the veil of blindness from Israel's eyes, and from the eyes of the Gentile church concerning Israel; this will bring forth a significant Awakening and great outpouring of the Holy Spirit, the fullness and completion of what began at Pentecost.

At the time that both the Foundation and the Cornerstone was laid, there were notable invasions of earth by Heaven, releasing great signs and wonders; the establishment of the Headstone and the release of the 'sons of God' will also come with a great invasion of earth and great signs in the Heavens and earth.

Israel is a both a natural and spiritual entity, a vessel that is progressively being transformed by God, from the natural into a Heavenly City (Gen. 22:17). Many look at Jerusalem with natural eyes and all they can see is a bloody City; it is time to begin to see with God's eyes; to understand with his heart, His passion for this nation, which has paid such a tremendous cost to be marked with His Name, from their conception to this present day.

It is important to challenge our beliefs and examine carefully in the Holy Spirit our doctrine concerning Israel, as Heaven begins to shine Light on the Word, releasing fresh revelation concerning Israel, for such a time as this.

> *"But now in Christ Jesus you who once were far away have been brought near through the blood of Christ. For he himself is our peace, who has made the two one and has destroyed the barrier, the dividing wall of hostility, by abolishing in his flesh the law with its commandments and regulations. His purpose was to create in himself one new man out of the two, thus making peace..."* *Ephesians 2:13-15 NIV*

On the Day of Pentecost the disciples who gathered together were in one accord; they were of one mind as they waited to receive the Promise of the Father spoken of by Jesus (Acts 1:4). Because of the unity amongst them, the disciples were positioned to receive the commanded blessing (Acts 1:14 2:1). God will command His blessing when we are of one accord once again.

> *"Behold, how good and how pleasant it is for brethren to dwell together in unity! It is like the precious oil upon the head, running down on the beard, the beard of Aaron, running down on the edge of his garments. It is like the dew of Hermon, descending upon the mountains of Zion; for there the LORD commanded the blessing— Life forevermore." Psalm 133*

God's view of union is portrayed by oil flowing down from the Head of Aaron—the high priest of Israel, down his beard to the edge of his priestly garments. Union of the Body of Christ cannot be accomplished until there is honor and union between Israel and the Gentile church, and Israel is restored to the place of the head and not the tail. The River flows from Heaven through Christ position in Jerusalem, and the oil flows from the Head of Christ through Israel to His Body.

The Lord's ultimate plan is that the Gentile Church work together with the Jewish servants of God, to see Israel restored and prepared as the Bride for her coming Bridegroom and King, *"...make straight in the desert a highway for our God" (Isaiah 40:3).*

> *"For I tell you that Christ has become a servant of the Jews on behalf of God's truth, to confirm the promises made to the patriarchs so that the Gentiles may glorify God for his mercy, as it is written: "Therefore I will praise you among the Gentiles; I will sing hymns to your name." Again, it says, "Rejoice, O Gentiles, with his people." Romans 15:8-12*

To everything, there is a season and a time for every purpose; the time has come for Jew and Gentile to work together to build the Temple of the Lord according to God's blueprint, and to bring in the Ark of His Presence.

In the same way that David made all the preparation and provisions for the building of the Temple of God, Jesus has made all the preparations and provision for the Temple to be completed. The stones have been prepared, the wood has been cut, the iron for the doors and gates is now ready; there is bronze, silver and gold in abundance, and the wine and the oil is prepared (1 Chronicles 22).

God has been at work preparing His skilled workers— Intercessors, leaders, churches and ministries: specialists in every field of building work, *"all types of skillful men"* and women, each one having their part to contribute, important the completion of the House. The wine and the oil are being prepared to be poured out, to sustain and equip all the workers to complete the building, and for the procession to bring the Ark of His Presence into the Sanctuary.

> *"Now set your heart and your soul to seek the LORD your God. Therefore arise and build the sanctuary of the LORD God, to bring the ark of the covenant of the LORD and the holy articles of God into the house that is to be built for the name of the LORD."* 1Chronicles:22:19

The enemies of God have been uniting against the Kingdom of God and have been gaining ground. The Body of Christ has proven to be very weak because of its many divisions. It is time to set our focus on the Father and submission to the Father's Will and the Father's ways, as the fullness of time for *the Father's* purposes and *the Father's* dreams has come. As Victor Hugo once said, *"Like the trampling of a mighty army, such is the force of an idea whose time has come."*

We are now approaching the time for the Father's dream of the completion of His House—the building of the Headstone; the time of the Father's dream for his daughters; the time of the revelation of the Sons of God; the time of the restoration of all things.

It is time for the fullness of the Father's Promise—*the commanded blessing*; the time of the *Day of His Power*—when His people volunteer freely. It is time for the day of the Harvest—the day of multitudes of harvesters being sent into the fields to bless the world in the Spirit of the Father.

It is time for the restoration of the nation of Israel and the Jewish people; the time for the Messiah's unveiling of Himself to them. It is the time for love and union in the Body of Christ, the time to end the night of wrong as stated by the poet William Merrill:

Rise up, O men of God! Have done with lesser things;
Give heart and mind and soul and strength to serve the King of Kings.
Rise up O men of God! His Kingdom tarries long;
Bring in the day of brotherhood and end the night of wrong.
Rise up O men of God!
The Church for you doth wait,
Her strength unequal to her task
RISE UP AND
MAKE HER GREAT

APPENDIX

ANTI-SEMITISM

&

CLEANSING PRAYER

ANTI-SEMITISM

Excerpted from 'The Plumb Line' by Faith Marie Baczko

The Almighty God of Heaven and Earth chose Israel as the nation through whom the whole counsel of God would be imparted and released as a blessing to the whole earth. The Patriarchs who are the fathers of God's work in man were all established in Israel. Through Israel, He blessed the earth with His Commandments and His Word, and through Israel He chose to take the form of a Jewish man who would give His life for the sins of the whole world. The Covenant and the promises were given to Israel, and through the Jewish King Jesus we as Gentiles are grafted in to Israel and get to partake of the fat of their root (Rom. 11:17).

> *"Theirs is the adoption as sons; theirs the divine glory, the covenants, the receiving of the law, the temple worship and the promises. Theirs are the patriarchs, and from them is traced the human ancestry of Christ, who is God over all, forever praised! Amen." Romans 9:4-5 NIV*

Anti-Semitism is in essence rebellion against God and is the anti-Christ spirit of Satan himself. It is a spirit that has become deeply rooted in the psyche of man throughout the nations of the world. This phenomenon exists in every nation because wherever there is rebellion against God, a covenant of agreement is entered into with Satan, the one who hates the nation of Israel and the Jewish people.

In seeking to preserve his rule and reign on earth, Satan's fierce determination is to remove any possibility of the return of the Jewish King Jesus, whose feet will once again stand on the soil of Israel from where His Kingdom will be administered (Is. 2:3, Zech14:6). Jesus' return signals the end of Satan's diabolic reign and his malevolent plan is to inspire all nations and peoples to turn against the Jewish people, destroy the nation of Israel altogether and prevent the return of Christ.

God declared in His word that if we choose to bless His people Israel, we would be blessed and partake of the His covenant with Israel and corresponding blessings through Jesus. He also pronounced a curse on all who hate, persecute and reject Israel, and therefore reject the blessings of Israel provided for them, *"I will bless those who bless you, And I will curse him who curses you; and in you* [Israel] *all the families of the earth shall be blessed" (Gen 12:3).*

In Deuteronomy chapters 28 to 30, God offered Israel the choice to be extravagantly blessed (36 blessing) through obedience to His commands, or to fall under a curse (169 curses) if they chose the path of rebellion. He also decreed that these *very same curses* would come upon all the nations who chose to curse and persecute Israel.

> *"I make this covenant and this oath, not with you alone, but with him who stands here with us today before the LORD our God, as well as with him who is not here with us today..." Deuteronomy 29:14*

> *"Also the LORD your God will put all these curses on your enemies and on those who hate you, who persecuted you." Deuteronomy 30:7*

Anti-Semitism can be traced throughout history and the generational lines through most cultures, nations and religions of the world. In World Wars I and II most nations took their stand against Israel which has continued to this very day through the United Nations. Most Religions, in their history, including the Roman Catholic Church, the Lutheran Church, and the Anglican Church, all took part in persecuting the Jewish people, some in horrific ways.

 Over one hundred cities or nations have expelled the Jewish people from their land since A.D. 250, including, France, Germany, England, Hungary, Switzerland, Belgium, Italy, Spain, Portugal, Ukraine and Russia and all Arab nations to name a few.   Before Christ—B.C., Most empires conquered and persecuted the Jewish people from the time God gave birth to Israel as nation. Both North and South America are comprised of people who came from Europe and other nations of the world – most people of the world are therefore from an ancestry line that has persecuted the Jewish people in some way, whether through their religion, their nation, or both, and therefore fall under these generational curses (see Number 14:18 Jdg. 6:25-26).

Reflection

Examine your heart and your family's for any mind-sets, attitudes, anger or offensive way toward the Jewish people.

Cleansing Prayer for Anti-Semitism
(Based on Deuteronomy 28)

O Lord God of Heaven, great and awesome God who keeps His covenant of unfailing love with those who love Him and obey His commands (Neh. 1). Lord you have chosen Israel to be a blessing to the nations of the world; they have paid the tremendous cost to give the world Your Word, Your commandments and ordinances, the revelation of Your Awesome Majesty, and they have suffered the travail to birth Your Son, the King of Kings and Lord of Lords—Jesus Christ. God of Abraham, Isaac and Jacob; Lord, You whose mercy endures forever, I and my forefathers have sinned against you and Your people Israel.

Lord, You said to Abraham, the father of Isaac and Israel, "I will bless those who bless you, and I will curse those who curse you." You said through Moses Your servant that You would inflict all the curses written in Deuteronomy 28 on Israel's enemies, and on those who hate and persecute Israel (Deut. 30:17).

Father God, I confess the sin of Anti-Semitism in my generational line, I confess that we have persecuted, mocked and cursed Your chosen people Israel.

Lord, I and my forefathers have rebelled and not obeyed Your Word to bless Your people and to pray for their peace, but have chosen to disobey your command to bless Israel and have cursed them with our judgments and the curses of our mouths; so now the solemn curses and judgments written in the law of Moses, the servant of God, have come upon us because of our sin against your people Israel .

Lord the forefathers of most nations have been found guilty of this anti-Semitic, anti–Christ spirit. Lord, I and my forefathers have allowed the

Anti-Christ spirit that hates Your Son Jesus, to use us to persecute Your Son and inflict the worst horrors on Your people Israel. Lord the blood of Your son Israel cries out from the land of the nations of the earth; forgive us for defiling the land with this most terrible and grievous sin.

Lord the fathers of the gentile church, birthed through Your Jewish Son Jesus, have sinned against Your people Israel, from its conception. Lord the fathers of the Roman Catholic Church, and the fathers of the Protestant, Lutheran and Anglican churches have committed grave sins of persecution, exile, murder and torture against your people Israel. O Lord the fathers of the gentile church have sinned against Your sons and daughters of Israel throughout history and in most nations even to this very day. O Merciful God we are covered in shame for our many sins and crimes against your people.

Lord, You said in Your Word that Your people Israel would be in the midst of many peoples like showers on the grass. Lord forgive us and all our ancestors from Spain, Portugal, Italy, Hungary, Austria, Lithuania, Russia, Ukraine, France, Germany, England, all Arab nations and all 109 cities and nations throughout the centuries who have exiled your people from land you placed them in as dew, to be a blessing, and left them homeless and destitute (Mic.5:7). O Lord forgive our sin!

Lord, in persecuting your son Israel we have persecuted your Jewish Son Jesus—the Lion of the tribe of Judah, who will return to establish His Kingdom on earth, as the Jewish King of Israel, whose centre is Jerusalem (Zech 14:6, Is, 2:3).

You have declared that Your Law shall go forth from Zion. Forgive us Lord for attempting to usurp their place of honor in Your kingdom. You declared Jerusalem to be an immovable rock and a heavy stone, that any who try to move it would be injured; forgive us and our forefathers for attempting to move Jerusalem's place of honor and replace it with Rome, Constantinople, St. Petersburg and with England (Zech. 12).

O Lord, You are gracious and merciful and anxious to pardon those who love you when we confess our sins, ask your forgiveness, repent and turn from our wicked way(Ps. 86:15)s.

O Lord, I come before Your Throne of Mercy and ask for Your forgiveness, Your pardon and Your cleansing from my sin and the sins of my fathers and all bloodguilt. We stand under the shadow of the Cross and plead the Blood of your Son Jesus.

When Jesus became a curse for us on the Cross, He nailed all decrees and the written requirements against us to the Cross and made a public spectacle and open show of Satan. Because all our sin including our sin against the Jewish people, were nailed to the Cross, I ask that You would pardon me and my family today and break all curses that have come upon us as a result of anti-Semitism.

I renounce the sin of anti—Semitism and choose to embrace Israel, the apple of Your eye, Your special treasure. I choose to bless and honor them as the patriarchs, the fathers of Your Church, to whom belong the Shekinah Glory, the covenants, the Law and the Promises (Rom. 9:4).

Cleanse me O Lord, and in your mercy wash the stain of this sin from my life and the lives of my children, and my children's children. Lord I ask that you would in your awesome might and power, please cleanse all land of any nation defiled by myself or my ancestors to a thousand generations from the sin of anti-Semitism and all the evil it has produced. Lord I plead the blood of Jesus over all defiled land and break all ties to defiled land today.

Lord remove the root from my family line and break the power of the sin of anti-Semitism over our lives today, and in Your great mercy and grace cancel the curses you pronounced on those who curse, persecute or harm Your chosen people.

Break the power of the curse on the fruit of the womb and of barrenness; the curse on our going out and coming in.

Break the power of the curse of confusion and the rebuke on everything we put our hand to, until we are destroyed and come to sudden ruin.

Break the power of the curse of a bronze sky over our head and iron ground beneath us. Lord break the curse of being defeated by our enemies and Yours.

Break the power of the curse of failure, oppression and robbery from our lives with no one to rescue. Break the curse of being the tail and not the head, of others lending to us but not being able to lend to others. Break the curse of debt and financial lack.

Lord, break the power of the curse of not being able to possess our harvest and keep it;

Break the power of the curse of disease, infirmity and sickness, wasting disease, fever, inflammation, boils, tumors, scurvy and itch, and diseases that cannot be cured. Incurable boils on legs and knees and from head to foot, severe and lingering diseases and prolonged disasters.

Break the power of the curse of an anxious mind, madness, blindness, panic and tragedy; eyes weary with longing and a despairing heart.

Break the power of the curse of defeat by our enemies

Break the power of the curse of oppression, robbery and loss

Break the power of the curse of slavery of my natural and spiritual children to their enemies and the yoke of captivity on their lives.

Break the power of the curse of being exiled on my generational line.

Break the power of the curse of mockery, ridicule and horror from my life and the life of my family.

Break the power of the curse of disease on the produce of our land.

Break the power of the iron yoke of oppression from our neck

Break the power of the curse of devouring our sons and daughters

Break the power of the curse of a cold heart and lack of love in our family

Break the power of the curse of plagues and unbearable sickness and all diseases.

Break the power of the curse of poor eyesight, trembling heart, a despairing soul and fear.

Lord by faith I now release myself from the grip of all demonic curses and command them to be gone now and forever from my life.

By faith, I now stand under the shadow of the Cross and claim the Power in the Blood of Jesus that was shed for me, I am cleansed, washed and sanctified by the Blood of Jeshua and His forgiveness of my sin.

I now declare *myself and my family to a thousand generations loosed from the spirit of anti-Semitism—the spirit of anti-Christ, and all accompanying curses through Jesus' victory and triumph at the cross.*

By faith, I now remove myself from the tainted bloodline of my ancestors and place myself and my children under the protection of the Blood of Jeshua, our Messiah. Lord I ask that You would remove, by Your Great Power, every trace of the anti-Semitic influence from my thinking processes, that the demonic veil covering my eyes concerning Israel would be removed, that I may see clearly and think righteously according to Your Word. Today I make the choice to bless Israel, I declare that their people are my people and their God is My God (Ruth1:16).

Lord I choose obedience to Your Word to be a blessing to Israel and to pray for the peace of Jerusalem until You make her a praise in the earth. Thank You LORD for the Blood that cleanses me. Amen

Prophecies Concerning Israel

Solomon's Temple Destroyed and Israel taken to Babylon in captivity – 605 BC

"Behold, I will send and take all the families of the north,' says the LORD, 'and Nebuchadnezzar the king of Babylon, my servant, and will bring them against this land, against its inhabitants, and against these nations all around, and will utterly destroy them, and make them an astonishment, a hissing, and perpetual desolations...And this whole land shall be a desolation and an astonishment, and these nations shall serve the king of Babylon seventy years. Then it will come to pass, when seventy years are completed, that I will punish the king of Babylon and that nation, the land of the Chaldeans, for their iniquity,' says the LORD; 'and I will make it a perpetual desolation." Jeremiah 25:9-11

"'They shall be carried to Babylon, and there they shall be until the day that I visit them,' says the LORD. Then I will bring them up and restore them to this place." Jeremiah 27:22

Israel re-gathered to the land to rebuild the Temple – 536 BC

"In the first year of Cyrus king of Persia, in order to fulfill the word of the LORD spoken by Jeremiah, the LORD moved the heart of Cyrus king of Persia to make a proclamation throughout his realm and also to put it in writing: "This is what Cyrus king of Persia says: "'The LORD, the God of heaven, has given me all the kingdoms of the earth and he has appointed me to build a temple for him at Jerusalem in Judah. Any of his people among you may go up to Jerusalem in Judah and build the temple of the LORD, the God of Israel, the God who is in Jerusalem, and may their God be with them." Ezra: 1-3

Destruction of the Zerubbabel's Temple – 70 AD

"Then Jesus went out and departed from the temple, and His disciples came up to show Him the buildings of the temple. And Jesus said to them, "Do you not see all these things? Assuredly, I say to you, not one stone shall be left here upon another, that shall not be thrown down." Matthew 24:1-2

Israel re-gathered to the land a second time to become a nation – 1948 AD

"It shall come to pass in that day that the Lord shall set His hand again the second time to recover the remnant of His people who are left, from Assyria and Egypt, from Pathros and Cush, from Elam and Shinar, from Hamath and the islands of the sea. He will set up a banner for the nations, and will assemble the outcasts of Israel, and gather together the dispersed of Judah from the four corners of the earth." Isaiah 11:11

"Therefore behold, the days are coming," says the LORD, "that it shall no more be said, 'The LORD lives who brought up the children of Israel from the land of Egypt,' but, 'The LORD lives who brought up the children of Israel from the land of the north and from all the lands where He had driven them.' For I will bring them back into their land which I gave to their fathers. Jeremiah 16:14-15

The New Temple to include Gentiles

"On that day I will raise up The tabernacle of David, which has fallen down, and repair its damages; I will raise up its ruins, and rebuild it as in the days of old; that they may possess the remnant of Edom, and all the Gentiles who are called by My name," Says the LORD who does this thing." Amos 9:11-12

Judgment on the nations in the last – 20?? AD

"For behold, in those days and at that time, when I bring back the captives of Judah and Jerusalem, I will also gather all nations, and bring them down to the Valley of Jehoshaphat; And I will enter into judgment with them there on account of My people, My heritage Israel, whom they have scattered among the nations; they have also divided up My land." Joel 3:1-2

"On that day I will set out to destroy all the nations that attack Jerusalem. And I will pour out on the house of David and the inhabitants of Jerusalem a spirit of grace and supplication. They will look on me, the one they have pierced, and they will mourn for him as one mourns for an only child, and grieve bitterly for him as one grieves for a firstborn son." Zechariah 12:9-10

"Then the LORD will go out and fight against those nations, as he fights on a day of battle. On that day his feet will stand on the Mount of Olives, east of Jerusalem, and the Mount of Olives will be split in two from east to west, forming a great valley, with half of the mountain moving north and half moving south." Zechariah 14:3-4

Related Scripture: Ezekiel 20:40-44, 34:11-30, 37:1-28, Isaiah 60:8-16, Hosea 3, 4,

ABOUT THE AUTHOR

In 1993 *Faith Marie Baczko* had a life transforming encounter with the Lord at her apartment in downtown Toronto. In obedience to the Lord, she walked away from her career as fashion designer, and the store she had recently opened in the heart of Toronto. When she asked the Lord what she would do, He said, *"Write."* Having no experience in writing, and no natural ability, something within Faith believed God and she chose to follow Him.

With her twelve year old son Jesse, Faith followed the Lord to a small village outside of Toronto. There the Lord began her training and cleansing in His refining fire, there also He began to teach her about His House, and the completing work on His House—the Headstone or Capstone.

After losing her son in a tragic car accident in 2006, the Lord gave Faith the gift of a partner and husband; she married Frank, and together they fellowship and minister at Catch the Fire Toronto. Shortly after their marriage they launched Headstone Ministries to facilitate their ministry to the Lord. Faith and Frank's passion is to see the House of God aligned to the Plumb line of Christ and for the saints to rise up to the fullness of their destiny in Christ, *to prepare the way of the LORD.*

Faith is a prophetic teacher, now speaking and ministering internationally in the Body of Christ. She is an ordained pastor through the Partners in Harvest Network of Churches. She has held many conferences & Seminars in South America and the Caribbean and her books and teachings are now all available in Spanish.

Having sat at the Lord's feet for many years receiving the revelation on the Headstone of the Temple of God, He has now released her to bring this timely word, to the Body of Christ. Like the women at the tomb, she has also received the command to, *"Go and tell..."* (Matt. 28).

Faith Marie Baczko is available to minister and to hold Schools & seminars focused on:

➢ The significance of Israel in God's purposes & plans
➢ The Significance of God's plan for women in the last days
➢ Becoming Ready as the Bride

For more Information please contact us at:

Headstone Ministries

1-312 Reynolds Street Oakville ON Canada L6J 3L8

Website: www.headstoneministries.com
Email: contact@headstoneministries.com

One United painting by Christine Peterkin – www.inspirationalart.ca
Israel My Son illustration by Martha Charlton

Publications in The Headstone Series:

The Plumb Line

The fullness of the Measure of the Stature of Christ

The Blueprint

God's Transcendent Plan of Redemption!

In His Image

In the Image of God He Created Them, Male & Female He Created Them!